When Students Grieve:

A Guide to Bereavement in the Schools

2nd Edition

By Alfred J. Liotta, Ed.D., M.S.W.

With a Foreword by Patrick M. Del Zoppo, Ph.D., C.A.S.
and Preface by Christopher Kilcullen, A.C.S.W.

LRP Publications
Horsham, Pennsylvania 19044
(215) 784-0860

Library of Congress Cataloging-in-Publication Data

Liotta, Alfred J.
    When students grieve : a guide to bereavement in the schools /
    by Alfred J. Liotta.
        p.   cm.
    Includes bibliographical references and index.
    ISBN 1-57834-036-5
    1. Teenagers and death. 2. Children and death. 3. Grief in adolescense. 4. Grief in children. 5. Bereavement in adolescence. 6. Bereavement in children. 7. Teenagers—Counseling of. 8. Children—Counseling of. I. Title.

BF724.3.D43L56 2003
155.9'37'083—dc21

                                        2003047718

The Second Edition of

When Students Grieve: A Guide to Bereavement in the Schools

is dedicated to

Salvatore Pagliaro, M.D.

Gordon Thornton, Ph.D.

Christopher Kilcullen, A.C.S.W.

Maxine Greene, C.S.W.

Four stars in a galaxy of friends

Everyone can master grief but he who has it.
— William Shakespeare

ABOUT THE AUTHOR

 **ALFRED J. LIOTTA, Ed.D., M.S.W.,** served in public education in New York City for 32 years and has written numerous manuals, curricula, and published articles. He is a Certified Pastoral Bereavement Counselor and was a parish and program facilitator in the Archdiocese of New York. He also is certified as a grief counselor by the international Association of Death Education and Counseling.

Dr. Liotta completed his M.S.W. degree at Fordham University and began to unite his educational career experience and counseling skills as an adolescent and family therapist.

Currently, he is a practicing school administrator and thanatologist and is active in church ministries. He is the coordinator of various bereavement ministries, as well as a bereavement consultant to Bennett Funeral Home in Scarsdale, N.Y. Dr. Liotta writes and lectures frequently. One of his most recent events was as a guest lecturer at Trinity College, in Dublin, Ireland.

Dr. Liotta maintains a bereavement counseling practice in the City of White Plains, New York. He is listed in *Who's Who in the East* and *Who's Who in Education* and is the recipient of numerous awards.

A native of Brooklyn, N.Y., Dr. Liotta is a seasoned educator, counselor and writer.

TABLE OF CONTENTS

FOREWORD

Change is the ever-present hallmark of adolescence. It is a time when autonomy is blossoming as well as a heightened control of self, others, and one's own environment.

It seems to be a time when all is well — at least for the time being. Adults looking back into the rear-view mirror might have forgotten the power generated from the toes on up that guided our thoughts, feelings and actions that occurred in one of the most reactionary times in our life.

Teen grief is a fresh wound without the onset of the healing scar. It is as powerful as the strongest of ocean waves upon the beach, and it occurs during a heightened time of life development when the adolescent has one foot in the world of childhood and another foot firmly planted in the onset of adulthood.

My initial work with teen loss occurred in 1990 following the tragic death of 89 young adults in an arsonist's fire in a Bronx, New York, night club ironically called *Happy Land*. The initial reaction of the hundreds of survivors during that late night and several days immediately thereafter was horror and fear muted by the shock. Our crisis intervention teams continued our pledge of support in the days, months and, in some cases, several years following the traumatic deaths.

As I watched the young survivors of the loss (in most cases sibling/peer loss), I was aware that regression and child-like behavior was a coping and defense mechanism unconsciously employed to provide elements of safety and respite. While denial was not the operative safety measure, a sense of respite (time for relief) was absolutely necessary. And of course, that respite was absolutely necessary because the young adult frame of mind cannot handle the enormous task of reality and confrontation in the immediate aftermath of loss and the effects of grief.

Let us consider that for many adolescents encountering loss, we are less than a decade away from a developmental time in life when death was considered a reversible process. For 13- or 14-year-olds, death was not permanent in their frame of reference until 6 through 7 years of age. Though real, it still was a far-off reality, and magical

xiii

thinking through restoration is still a possibility until close to 10 years of age. Bereavement Caregivers must look at loss in their own rear-view mirror and their own ongoing developmental process. Adolescent loss is a loss that must be nurtured in its healing journey. Confrontation with the fragile young griever requires a relationship of trust to be established over a period of time. And when time is a crucial factor, especially in crisis intervention, provision for safety, honesty and some sense of control are key elements of the helping alliance with adolescent mourners.

Dr. Alfred Liotta invites the Bereavement Helper to enter the delicate time of grief in a teen's life as a befriender of the loss process. His encouragement of bereavement knowledge provides us with a reality that will impart control and management of reality into the teen's world of loss and recovery. In adolescent loss, control and management are key areas of coping skills that do not imply denial, but rather a necessary and complementary task objective that is a pathway to increasing coping skills and coping realities. Teens discard artificial advice and step-by-step process-solving techniques. Teens feel pain and want to address it, or at least be provided with self-skills to be able to address the pain. Dr. Liotta addresses grief and its aftermath as a reality called "pain and hurt" that must be *understood* and *expressed* during an ongoing time of confrontation. Its invitation to "expression" is a key area for the caregiver's ongoing development. Most caregiver's will consider a quick journey through the pain since pain is a difficult exhibition of our wounds. And here, falling back into childhood expression of wound exhibition is a necessity.

When adolescent wounds are exhibited publicly, a sense and forum of safety must be provided to allow feelings to be understood, confronted and eventually expressed. In this sense, *When Students Grieve* rightfully places safety into peer and collaborative forums such as the adolescent bereavement support network. These peer-centered support programs provide the elements of safety and security, and foster adolescent developmental needs such as recognition and response during the healing journey. While these supportive networks are not therapy or cure-alls, they provide *empathy* and *hope*, which Dr. Liotta rightfully claims as necessary ingredients along the teen's personal and ongoing road to recovery.

It is refreshing to see such models of supportive educational networking through a multi-disciplinary approach to teen care-giving. Dr. Liotta has given the helping alliance a fine working model easily integrated into school and community systems that see themselves as wholesome agents of change and recovery when teens face loss.

— Patrick Michael Del Zoppo, Ph.D., C.A.S.
  Clinical Thanatologist

xv

PREFACE TO SECOND EDITION

When Students Grieve, hailed by Dr. Patrick Del Zoppo, in the foreword he wrote for the first edition of this book, as a "fine working model," has weathered the storm and has proven to be a valuable asset to caretakers and counselors in their efforts to provide the empathy, direction, and hope that people so desperately need in their journey through grief and along their road to recovery.

When Alfred J. Liotta, Ed.D., M.S.W., a seasoned writer, educator and counselor penned the first edition, it soon became obvious that he was presenting a well-prepared and well-thought-out protocol for grief counseling. It was current, it was concise, and above all, it was efficacious. It met the needs of the day admirably.

On Sept. 11, 2001, a new dawn shone forth on America. It was not expected, not well received, and not at all understood. While the reality of death had not changed, it was the manner of delivery that "rocked" the country and shocked the world. The gentle, pleasant complacency of American society had been shattered. America was attacked! The carnage defied belief. A new challenge in grief resolution was born.

What was terrorism? What was its impact? Why all this depression? How do we handle it? These were some of the questions confronting the scores of counselors who raced to the scenes. Where were the answers?

Again, Dr. Liotta took up pen to help make sense of it all, taking great pains to make sure this edition would offer some of the answers. Additions, amplifications, research and explanations have been incorporated into this second edition in an effort to ensure that the journey toward the resolution of grief continues to be as meaningful and effective as possible.

The reader will find that the new materials on "Terrorism" and "Depression" are essential additions that clearly present current factors that affect not only grief resolution, but also the entire comprehension of just what happened. In addition, the reader is specifically oriented to the various directions and waypoints that must be traveled during the survivor's journey.

In addition, this second edition provides the reader with an explanation and description of a common phenomenon known as "Disenfranchised Grief," which, in the past, has robbed countless troubled mourners of the opportunity to jointly and publicly participate in the acceptance and resolution of their grief.

The reader will be pleased to find that a modest amount of repetition has been deliberately employed to make this edition a bit more "user-friendly."

Due to the frequent referral to various items and concepts, Dr. Liotta has selectively repeated these items to provide ease and continuity in reading.

Consequently, *When Students Grieve, Second Edition*, is being presented to you as an updated, comprehensive, and versatile adjunct to the wonderful work that you are doing for others.

Read it. Enjoy it. Use it!

— Christopher Kilcullen, A.C.S.W.

ACKNOWLEDGEMENTS

The writing of this book could hardly be considered finished without words of thanks to my wife, Marie Elena, my daughter, Jennifer, and the many friends and acquaintances who have generously contributed to its ultimate completion. This nucleus of support both encouraged and convinced me of the timeliness and importance of the material gathered with respect to the field of bereavement counseling.

First, I must thank those individuals to whom this work is dedicated. Without their inspiration, guidance, and support this project would never have materialized. Their influence gave birth to not only a book, but, indeed, to a new career as well.

I also must thank George Shapiro, himself a bereaved spouse, Ann Marie and Vincent Ciaramella, Betty Skaggs, and Reverend Gerard Rafferty, all of whom were instrumental in keeping this project alive within me. Their encouragement and faith in the efficacy of the bereavement process became a mandate for me to complete the writing.

A special thank you must be given to Dan Mizroch, a bereaved parent, as well as to Gene Guarino and Tony Santelli who have each, in their own way, facilitated my writing.

Throughout my entire project, certain individuals have repeatedly voiced their faith in my ability to bring this contribution to fruition. In addition to my nuclear family, I owe a special thanks to Barbara Stevenson, Thelma Baxter, and Drs. Joseph Pedulla and Salvatore Pagliaro.

A special thanks also is due to my teacher, mentor, and friend, Patrick M. Del Zoppo, who has revitalized me in my middle years like the mythical Phoenix and inspired me to new heights of learning and service.

Finally, I would be pitifully remiss if I were not to thank the numerous grievers who allowed me the privilege of sharing each of their burdens and experiences. I hope that I have helped them nearly as much as they have helped me.

All of these people have truly been "the wind beneath my wings."

— Alfred J. Liotta

INTRODUCTION

In the many years that the author has worked with his students, he often has had occasion to share their joys as well as their sorrows, fears, and frustrations. It has always been gratifying for him to be allowed to share, and perhaps touch, their lives in some special way. It also has been difficult. To be asked for help at times when, perhaps, there are no answers; perhaps there are none available or none acceptable is no easy task. It is this difficulty, this vacuum created, that inspired the writing of *When Students Grieve* and this second edition that incorporates new grievance issues. This project was undertaken to facilitate better answers and a better process for those youngsters and their families who flounder in an emotional sea when confronted with the loss of a loved one.

When faced with a bereavement situation, one must have a prescribed format or protocol to pursue. The initial part of this protocol is the recognition of normal symptomatology as well as the knowledge of how to go about guiding the bereaved through the emotional labyrinth to the desperately sought acceptance and healing.

The steps to be followed, the questions to be asked, and the concepts to be pondered are all necessary components of the grief process or "journey."

Certain aspects of grief that are age-specific or mode-specific must be included in the overall process. Emotional considerations also must be explored as they may persist long after the funeral and the mourning have occurred.

Lastly, the way that one can adequately and properly memorialize the beloved with dignity and respect is an important consideration.

When considered and prioritized, all of these components provide the basic framework for *When Students Grieve.*

The book is designed to conform to this framework in a realistic and effective way. It begins with giving the reader an insight into some of the varied reactions that are to be expected and that are perfectly normal in a bereavement situation. This is followed by sample bereavement programs that can be offered to both students and parents. Special attention is given to an ordered exploration of specific determinants of grief as well as a discussion of crucial tasks of grief that are to be accomplished in the journey toward healing.

The center portion of the book deals with two specific age groups of young people — children and adolescents — and how each individual group has its own problems and considerations to be explored. Each group is provided with suggested intervention strategies. Throughout the text, periodic admonitions are given to alert counselors as to when certain behaviors or conditions warrant referral to professional mental health practitioners for appropriate treatment.

The latter part of the work is devoted to several informational considerations of selected topics that are of particular importance to contemporary bereavement situations. Suicide, homicide, anger, and guilt are each considered to bring its own unique set of problems and pressures to bear upon the successful resolution of the bereavement process or "journey."

In this second edition, we also examine the effects of terrorism (see Chapter 10), which has had a detrimental effect on society and brought to surface many emotions such as vulnerability, insecurity and fear. A final consideration is given to the purpose and kinds of memorialization that are available to survivors. This is an important consideration in that it generally is recognized as the first step in the acceptance and resolution of the loss.

Finally, the purpose of the book is to inform and guide school authorities and counseling personnel in providing viable and effective interventions when faced with death within the school community. The author offers logistical and procedural advice as to how selected interventions should be performed. In addition, there is an informative component whose purpose is to provide background information and danger signs for the counselors who may be less experienced with this area of intervention(s). The ultimate purpose of this work is to enable any given school to provide some measure of consolation, relief, hope, and direction to those young people and their families who languish in the pain of grief in their efforts to sort out answers. This book will help those who use it to meet that challenge.

CHAPTER 1

Reactions That May Accompany Uncomplicated, or Normal, Grief

I. Introduction

Perhaps the saddest and most emotionally and psychologically draining of all death experiences are those surrounding the loss of young people. Counselors and clinicians often rush to provide comfort and solace to survivors who are grappling with an assortment of conflicting and often disabling emotions.

Both counselors and laymen must remember that the grieving process frequently can involve feelings such as agitation, disorganization, restlessness, confusion, and impatience.[1] When confronted with these emotions, survivors frequently experience heightened anxiety simply because they are experiencing new and "different" feelings and begin to fear that they are becoming mentally ill. One researcher referred to this as the "Going crazy syndrome."[2]

While some of the behaviors that may accompany grief reactions can be upsetting, the counselor must recognize and explore the feelings with the survivors to assure them that these feelings are to be expected and are normal in the initial stages of the grieving process. While the astute counselor must be attentive to validating survivors' feelings, he or she also must be attuned to their fears and assure them that their sanity is not necessarily in question. Wolfelt encourages the griever, stating that: "[d]isorganization and confusion are actually stepping stones on your path toward healing."[3]

To better focus this discussion, a sample listing of common reactions that accompany the experience of normal, or uncomplicated, grief is provided by Patrick Del Zoppo. This listing will help both counselor and client better understand the emotional dynamics that interplay during the grieving process.

While a quick glance at the many behaviors may give rise to immediate concern for the survivor's mental stability, it must be clearly understood that these reactions are considered perfectly *normal* within the parameters of the normal, or uncomplicated, grief experience.

It is essential that the counselor identify these reactions and use his or her skills to validate feelings to start the survivor(s) on the road

1

toward healing. The key ingredients are the counselor's knowledge, skill, patience, empathy, understanding, and support. The client must know that he or she has a right to these feelings; it is normal; it is natural; and it is the beginning of a journey that will bring thoughts of the loved one from a piercing pain to a cherished memory.

Reactions in the Normal Grief Experience[4]

- Physical complaints
- Behavioral changes
- Changes in emotions and thought processes
- Interpersonal and social changes

I. Physical Sensations
hollowness in stomach
tightness in the chest
tightness in the throat
oversensitivity to noise
sense of depersonalization
breathlessness
weakness in muscles
lack of energy
dry mouth

II. Behaviors
sleep disturbances
appetite disturbances
absent-minded behavior
social withdrawal
dreams of the deceased
avoiding reminders of the deceased
searching and calling out
sighing
restless overactivity
crying
visiting places/carrying objects of value to the deceased
treasuring objects of the deceased

III. Feelings
anxiety/fear
loneliness
fatigue
shock
yearning
emancipation
relief
numbness
helplessness

IV. Cognitions
disbelief
confusion
preoccupation
sense of presence
hallucinations

II. Bereavement Program for Students

When school children, as well as adults, are confronted with the death of a friend or loved one, they frequently are left in a state of emotional, and even physical, turmoil (as evidenced by the preceding list of normal reactions). When the loss is of schoolwide proportion, school officials can be left in a tenuous state of turmoil as well. It falls to the officials to have a carefully devised and effective intervention plan in place to adequately deal with the needs of their student body. Often, this must be accomplished within the parameters of very demanding time constraints (usually immediately!).

One researcher speaks of the necessity to determine a "degree of trauma,"[5] in essence, to make an assessment of the extent to which a loss may impact the student body. The criteria are similar to the "determinants of grief," which will be discussed in this section and more completely in Chapter 3. School officials should carefully consider these criteria in order to get a realistic "reading" of the extent of the grief reaction, the size of the population to be counseled, and the elements of the school bereavement plan that should be used or, if appropriate, deleted.

This chapter focuses on the actual intervention plan for the grieving students. Any such plan requires the consideration of several components.

Facilities. In its overall bereavement or loss intervention plan, the school should have designated physical facilities earmarked for immediate use in the event that a loss of life, school emergency situation should develop. These facilities should be readily available for staff meetings, individual and group counseling, and parent briefing and counseling. Rooms or areas should be preassigned and ready for immediate use, for example, principal's briefing: Conference Room A; Bereavement Team orientation: Room 221; Parents' briefing: Auditorium. These assignments must be designated in a permanent plan. This type of coordination is not something that an experienced administrator or school Program Chairman would want to implement in the "heat of the moment." Prior planning, with designations on file, is strongly recommended. When news of a tragedy arrives, school personnel do not have time to plan, they must act!

Staff. While there is no question that members of the school staff are there primarily out of their love and concern for children, it must

3

be recognized that not everyone is prepared to give the particular and specialized guidance needed in a tragic/grief situation. Every educator and staff member will want to soften the hurt and reduce the pain. Yet all too often, well-meaning but inappropriate clichés in the hands of the untrained can be counterproductive or even detrimental. For this reason, a carefully selected, skilled team of counselors must be organized.

This "School Bereavement Team" should consist of the following knowledgeable individuals:

- School Psychologists

- Certified Bereavement Counselors

- Clinical Social Workers

- Board of Education Bereavement Specialists

- Qualified Guidance Counselors

This team, composed of counseling specialists, will be well equipped with the technical skills necessary to implement the procedures that are discussed below.

Materials. In addition to the face-to-face, interpersonal counseling that the school bereavement team can provide, a variety of helpful, supplemental materials should be available for students to use and/or borrow.

- Facial Tissues, Cups, Water, Juice, Coffee

- Appropriate Readings

- Poetry Selections

- Fact/Guidance Sheets

- Pertinent Periodical Articles

All the amenities of a comfortable counseling environment should be provided to the extent possible.

Resources. Many commercially prepared texts, articles and theme-specific periodicals are available. A library containing these materials should be established for both immediate and long-term use. (See the Bibliography in the back of this book for a list of excellent materials.)

Another resource that may be available to the school community is the use of local clergy and/or other community-based support groups. It would be wise, however, for school officials to check with the legal desk at the district office and with municipal officials before involving external assistance. Policies, legalities, and liabilities will vary from district to district.

Parental Notification. As with many other types of extra-curricular and co-curricular activities, bereavement counseling should be accompanied by some form of written, parental notification and written consent. Parents should be made aware that counseling will be available and give consent for their child to attend. Counseling should not be offered to students who lack parental permission.

Parents (or students) have the right to inspect and give written consent to school districts for all instructional material used in connection with any research or experimental program or project that involves their child.[6] Arguably, the type of activity that would involve school counseling in a loss of life situation, particularly in the case of a student passing away on school property or a student being attacked on school property, could fall within the ambit of The Protection of Pupil Rights Amendment Act (PPRA). As such, instead of consent being more or less permissive, it is strongly urged that parents be informed of the existence of the Bereavement Team and written advance consent be received.

The PPRA regulations apply to any program receiving federal funds for which the Secretary of Education is responsible; to any survey, analysis, or evaluation conducted in public schools; to any instructional materials (including supplemental materials). Psychiatric or psychological examination or test means a method of obtaining information, including a group activity, not directly related to academic instruction and designed to elicit information about attitudes, habits, traits, opinions, beliefs, or feelings.[7] Psychiatric or psychological treatment also is defined.[8]

The regulations require school districts to notify parents and students of their rights and mandates the Secretary of Education to enforce the statute. They also establish an office and review board to investigate, process, review, and adjudicate violations of the statute.

School officials should remember that:

1. Parents should be notified that bereavement counseling will be available.

2. Parents should be notified in writing that their child wishes to participate in bereavement counseling.

3. Parent consent slips should be signed, returned to the school, and kept on file.

Again, school officials are reminded to consult with local authorities to avoid legal complications. Generic, sample letters of parental notification and permission are included in Appendix A and Appendix B.

Procedures. When developing the "protocol" of bereavement counseling interventions, school officials should implement several important procedures and considerations to help the bereaved on their journey through grief.

1. *Counselors and clients should be able to meet in a quiet, comfortable, and uninterrupted setting.*

2. *Counselors should take the time to explain to the client just what grief is and what the bereavement process entails.*

Grief, basically, is a response to loss. It is often both physical and emotional in nature.[9] "Mourning," often used synonymously with grief, is technically when grief has gone public. (For example, during the actual time of the funeral, wearing black or whatever one's cultural mourning color may be, and cultural mourning periods.) It is a time of highly charged emotions.

Shock is nature's own emotional anesthesia and it often accompanies grief. Shock controls the balance of how much reality an individual can absorb at any given time. Shock can be very uncomfortable since it is a type of buffer that can shut out reality. Frequently, clients are known to have no recollection of who told them the news of the death or of certain events that occurred during the wake or the funeral. One researcher speaks of the woman who called shock a "little gift" that got her through something that would have been impossible for her to fully realize.[10]

Denial is the experience that often follows shock. It is a reaction that denies the loss. It produces in the survivor a sense of unreality: "it didn't happen," "it's just a bad dream." Eventually, with time, the survivor will come to both an intellectual and emotional awareness of the reality of the loss and begin to integrate its acceptance."[11]

3. *To be an effective component in the healing process, the astute counselor must both understand and explain the grieving process in terms of a "journey" to be taken.* The survivor(s) must be helped to confront the reality of the loss — that it has indeed occurred. Unfortunately, one cannot circumvent the process or the pain. One must go through the grieving, experience the pain of the loss, and feel the anger, confusion, disillusionment, and assortment of feelings that accompany the grieving process. The counselor is there to help the survivor manage the devastating emotional impact of the loss, as well as assist in bringing thoughts of the deceased from a piercing pain to a cherished memory.[12] This can only be done with great patience, sympathy, and empathic listening, and through a thorough exploration of the *determinants* and *tasks* of grief.

While the determinants and tasks of grief will be discussed in detail in Chapters 3 and 4, it is useful to at least highlight their major components at this point. This summary will reappear in Chapter 2 to facilitate matters for counselors whose purpose may be to focus solely on the parental segment of the grieving population.

In order to fully comprehend the extent of the loss, it is necessary for the survivor(s) to put into perspective just who the deceased was — Who in the life cycle has died? The nature of the attachment and the quality of the relationship must be explored. How the victim died will be an indicator of survivor grief as will certain historical antecedents, such as how the survivor resolved previous losses, his or her mental state, and existing life crises at the time of the death. The survivor's personality is also a determinant to be explored. Age, sex, the ability to express oneself, and the ability to handle anxiety and stress are all important factors in one's ability to grieve normally.[13]

Once the determinants of grief have been sufficiently explored, the skilled counselor can personalize and tailor interventions to usher

7

the survivor through the tasks to be accomplished for successful healing. These tasks must be accomplished for the survivor to reestablish equilibrium and to complete the process of mourning.[14]

One researcher outlines four basic tasks of grief to be accomplished.[15] The survivor(s) must first "accept the reality of the loss." No progress can be made when one is in denial. Once the death is acknowledged, the survivor(s) can move on to the next task, which is "to experience the pain of the grief." One must be prepared to experience the pain of the grief and not try to avoid it. Avoidance would only be a negation of this task and would be counterproductive.

Once the survivor has accepted the reality of the loss and has experienced the pain of the grief, he or she must "adjust to an environment in which the deceased is missing." To do this, the mourner must determine just *what* is missing and may have to assume some or all of the roles played by the deceased. The successful adaptation of these roles can be a turning point in grief resolution.

The final task of grief is "to withdraw the emotional energy invested in this relationship and reinvest it in another." The mourner must realize the need to withdraw the emotional energy that was invested in the relationship with the deceased and learn to let go without guilt. The mourner must then reinvest this energy in other relationships, indeed, in life itself.[16]

III. Effective Bereavement Counseling

If the school is to have an effective program in bereavement counseling, the counseling staff must know how to be effective counselors, understand how this type of counseling is conducted, and appreciate a viable therapeutic relationship with their clients.

In bereavement intervention, the counselor must be prepared to "meet the clients where they are." The counselor must be able to deal with the clients at their present stage of the journey, to explore and evaluate feelings, and to assess the survivors' backgrounds, relationships, and abilities to handle the grief they are confronted with.

The counselor must be patient, supportive, and empathic. He or she must make every effort to validate clients' feelings and must avoid well-meaning, but nonproductive, clichés that can actually negate rather than validate feelings. It is most essential that the bereaved be allowed to verbalize their feelings and be able to tell, and retell their story. This is part of the work of the second task of grief.

The following chart provides a finely tuned synthesis of the elements involved in effective bereavement counseling.[17]

Effectiveness of Bereavement Counseling

A. Effective Counselors are:

   1. Warm and sensitive to others.

   2. Open to their experience as well as to the experience of others.

   3. Able to listen with understanding.

   4. Able to communicate a sense of understanding to others.

   5. Nonjudgmental

   6. Able to respond flexibly.

B. How Counseling Works:

   1. The counseling takes place at a *critical time* in the life of another.

   2. The client *needs to gain understanding/insight* into this time.

   3. The client seeks ways of coping (that are usually established already in life context but may need modification).

   4. The counselor observes coping patterns:

      • Confront the situation.

      • Call out to another.

      • Comfort self physically.

      • Comfort self alone.

C. The Importance of the Therapeutic Relationship:

   1. Remember your responsibility for confidentiality

2. Be realistic about your level of competence.

3. Be aware of your limits regarding moral questions that you may ask your clients in order to get to know them or to help them.

4. Always self-evaluate yourself as to technique.

5. Never let your professional development/growth stop.

6. Be cautious about personal involvement.

7. Be aware of your own value judgments and how they relate to your work with your clients.

8. Recognize your client's own inner resources for solving and future ability to solve problems.

9. Review your services for comprehensiveness.

10. Never fail to appreciate the inherent dignity and worth of every human being you meet.

A. Bereavement Support Group

In establishing a viable, effective and complete school-based bereavement program, school officials must make provisions for corporate (group) interventions as well as for individual counseling. In the midst of the turmoil and emotional intensity that accompany the grief experience, the presence of others with similar concerns provides the survivor with a real dimension of security, acceptance, order, hope, and reality. The group may provide the survivor with the necessary support that may be absent in his or her own social system.[18] Other researchers also acknowledge the benefits of self-help groups. The exchange of mutual concerns and the release of feelings with others can stimulate and foster the healing process. This social and verbal interaction can result in new and valuable insights into problem resolution. Communication is seen as a vehicle to keep the bereaved in tune with those around them.[19]

Another researcher views the support group as a medium for providing a sense of community, safety, and opportunities for growth that will take the griever beyond the sorrow and the pain. He suggests that the bereavement support group have a threefold structure, with a protocol that should include *goals*, *procedures*, and a *10-session agenda*.[20]

It must be kept in mind, however, that the major function of the bereavement support group is to provide a measure of personal hope and support for the survivors as they struggle to adapt to their loss. These types of groups are neither therapy nor cure-alls. They are essentially mutual self-help groups led by an experienced facilitator. The underlying purpose, as in individual counseling, is to facilitate the journey from grief to healing. This can be accomplished via the threefold protocol.

Goals

1. Acceptance

Group members are encouraged to tell and retell their stories and to describe and share their fears, pains, and frustrations with others.

2. Understanding

Members are assured that their grief reactions and feelings are normal and that their mental stability is not in question. They develop a realization that others have had similar feelings and also have survived.

3. Growth

Members are guided toward evaluating the appropriateness of their own decisions and are encouraged to explore new and effective coping skills.

4. Safety

Members receive and share encouragement. They learn to cherish memories of their loved one(s) and develop the strength to say good-bye.

Procedures

To implement the goals and effectively carry out the program of the 10-session support group formats, it is necessary to establish certain specific procedures.

1. Admission to the Group

As pointed out earlier, admission to the group should be based on parental notification and written parental consent.

Referrals can come from individuals, staff members, administration, or parents.

In some instances, arranging a personal interview between the potential client and a counselor prior to admission to the group may be helpful to determine appropriateness of the particular group being offered.

Note: Counselors must exercise great care in the following situations:

- If a survivor is already in treatment with a health-care professional, he or she should be admitted to the group only with the approval of that therapist.

- If a survivor's needs are considered to be beyond the scope of what is available at the school level, he or she should not be permitted to join the group. The astute counselor will make every effort to provide an appropriate referral for that person.[21]

2. Criteria for Inclusion in Group

Membership in the school-based bereavement support group should be based on the following criteria:

- Survivors must have experienced the loss by death of a friend or loved one.

- Survivors should be ready to enter the journey toward healing "process." They must have moved beyond the point of numbness and shock

- Survivors must not be substance abusers.

- Survivors must not be exhibiting the symptoms of complicated grief.[22] These individuals must be referred to professional mental health therapists.

3. Group Composition

While many bereavement support groups may include members who have experienced different death circumstances — spouse, father, grandparent — due to a variety of factors, the school-based bereavement support group usually is composed of survivors of a "same-loss" (for example, everyone experienced the death of a student, or beloved staff member).

Under optimum conditions, the group size should range from five to 12 members. If co-facilitators are available, additional members can be added.

4. Contracting

One researcher views the contract as a vehicle to foster communication as well as to stimulate commitment.[23] It can be useful in the identification and commitment to the specific needs and concerns of the entire group. While contracts can take various forms, the important point is that they can be flexible and re-negotiated. In addition, the contract can be used to establish a sort of common denominator that reflects the mutual concerns of the participants.[24] In the school-based bereavement support group, the contract should include the following:

1. Basic limitations:

   a. **Time** — number and length of sessions

   b. **Confidentiality** — what can and cannot be discussed outside of the group

2. Mutually agreed-upon goals

3. Openness of communication

4. Extent of sharing of individual needs and wants

5. Need for mutual respect and acceptance devoid of judgmental reactions

5. Structure and Format of Meetings

The following operational components should be included in order to provide organization and consistency throughout the sessions.

- Suggested length of session — one and one-half hours in duration
- Initial lecture and review of previous work done
- Information-gathering and group feedback
- Use guest speakers; involves selection and evaluation
- Distribution of "homework" assignments or activities
- Pre- or post-session informal, community time with refreshments

6. Post-Intervention

Some form of follow-up activity should be included within the group procedures.

1. Follow-up note after initial session
2. Periodic communication throughout the year

Once the goals and procedures have been established for the school bereavement support group, the counselor should now turn his or her attention to the composition of the individual sessions themselves. While groups may meet an average of eight to 12 sessions, a midpoint, 10-session format will be presented as a model protocol.

The 10-Session Model Agenda

During the course of the group sessions, the school-based support group will exist as a mini-community replete with its own common goals, experiences, and needs. In order to foster the necessary intimacy, trust, understanding, and healing, the following agenda is suggested.

Session 1. Getting Acquainted

The initial session should be used to give group members the opportunity to become acquainted with each other and with the group leader (facilitator). It is an opportunity for group members to be exposed, perhaps for the first time, to the language of loss. This session should be used to develop an understanding and awareness that the purpose of the group is for self-help and not for therapy. The opening session also should be used to establish the group climate: developing the contract, norms, mutual respect, and an understanding of the role of the group leader.

Session 2. Members Experience the Loss

Group members are asked to share with the group why this particular loss experience brought them to this group and how the loss affected them. It is an opportunity for the group members, as well as for the facilitator, to learn something about each member's loss experience. It also is an opportunity for the exploration of common experiences and loss reactions. This session can provide the opportunity for members to explore instances of past loss and healing encounters in the survivors' lives.

Session 3. Reactions of Shock, Disbelief and Denial

Group members are asked to share their feelings of shock at the announcement that the loss actually happened. The facilitator can explore the nature and purpose of shock. Feelings of disbelief and the common psychological defense mechanism known as "denial" can be discussed and explained. Eventually, with intellect and reality testing, the events surrounding the loss will be understood. Effective bereavement counseling deals with the death event itself as the survivor begins to integrate the story into the present reality. Storytelling can be used to enhance reality as the survivor's reactions and the events of the death are both felt and understood. There should be continuous group discussion, and the group leader can maximize this by using leading questions and selected exercises. Showing of personal pictures and videos can be meaningful activities. Expression of feelings should be encouraged, and members must be assured that tears are a normal, important part of the healing process.

Session 4. Understanding Normal (Uncomplicated) Grief

The facilitator should explain grief simply as a response to a loss — it is normal and appropriate. The group should consider each of the physical, emotional, behavioral, and cognitive reactions that accompany the grieving process. The facilitator may wish to develop hand-outs for group members to use to express themselves as they come to the awareness and understanding of how normal their feelings really are.

Session 5. Post-Loss Feelings and Emotional Reactions

Group members should consider that the common denominator of the grieving process is the pain; grief hurts. Survivors must realize that while they may experience strange and unusual feelings, it is normal, even expected. What may differ among the individuals is the frequency of the reactions, as well as the duration and intensity. The central focus of this session should be to have group members openly share these feelings. An important part of this session is for group members to realize their normalcy and put aside their feelings of "going crazy."

Session 6. Grief Work with Difficult Reactions

Group members should briefly review the many unusual feelings they have discussed and may have experienced. They should develop an awareness of the times they opted to suppress these feelings because of their unique strangeness. It is important that the survivors realize that one cannot simply choose to "go around" these feelings. The grief experience must be felt at its peak of intensity before it can significantly subside. The griever must work through the grief within the parameters of the emotional, social, and cultural support systems available to him or her. Social integration and cultural adaptations can reinforce this support.

Session 7. Dealing with Secondary Losses

Group members will discuss the unique quality of the relationship they enjoyed with the deceased. Each relationship was characterized by special roles, such as a tutor or a gym partner. These roles no longer exist as a result of the death of the friend or loved one. Their loss also will result in a particular grief reaction. Group members must share their feelings in order to accommodate the loss and make the necessary adjustment. Often, one is not totally aware of these special roles until confronted with the void that is created. The group leader should assist members in discussing these secondary losses and ways of accommodating them.

Session 8. From Emptiness to New Beginnings

Group members will discuss their individual feelings of sadness and loneliness. They should be encouraged to openly express how and why they miss their friend or loved one and why such a "vacuum" is left in their lives. The group leader may give a written exercise in which each member can identify ways of beginning anew or reinvesting the emotional energy from the old relationship into a new one. These expressions and ideas can be shared, compared, and integrated into a new beginning.

Session 9. The Cherished Memory

Memories, both good and bad, can be powerful feelings. The facilitator can give the group an oral exercise in which members can expand on memories of their loved one. Verbalization is quite beneficial and is part of how an individual "tells his story." The recollection of so many wonderful times can usher in a new relationship with the friend or loved one, that of a cherished memory.

Session 10. A Time for Closure and Personal Evaluation

Group members will review their experience, the reactions they had, the skills they learned, and the feelings they explored. Time should be given to address any individual or group needs that were not met by the group. The facilitator should provide time for members to say goodbye to each other and to share their evaluation of their progress and expectations. This can be an emotional, yet very powerful, experience.[25]

IV. Effective Actions for School Officials

When faced with a loss of life event or a crisis, school officials can suddenly find themselves severely encumbered by time-constraints, logistics, and procedures to be followed. This chapter was designed to help ease that burden.

Today's school officials are well-trained and experienced educational personnel. They are aware that different situations call for different procedures. Similarly, not all death events within the school community are the same; some are more devastating than others, some may be more expected than others. Consequently, not all procedures are required, or even desirable, in all situations. Martha Oates compiled an unusually comprehensive and well-organized "Action

Checklist" that is excellent for school bereavement contingencies.[26] Depending on the circumstances, school officials can select or delete items to tailor the required procedures to the situation.

School officials must remember, however, that procedures, legalities, and liabilities may vary from venue to venue. A quick call to the legal desk at the Central Office is advised.

Action Checklist

_____1. The principal notifies the district's school superintendent or other designated central office staff person (unless notification of the death came from central office personnel).

_____2. The principal notifies the crisis team, key campus personnel, and appropriate central office personnel (e.g., student intervention coordinator, public information officer, or psychologist) of the death. The principal sets a time and place for these individuals to meet. Depending on the time available, this group may accomplish some or all of the following tasks:

- Meet individually or in small groups with teachers who will be personally affected by the death. Schedule a faculty meeting and notify all teachers and staff of the death and the time and place of the meeting.

- Arrange for substitutes for some teachers, if warranted, and advise them of the faculty meeting. Substitutes who are familiar with the school may serve as "rovers" to relieve any teacher who is grieving or who needs a break.

- Prepare announcements to be read to students, a script for those who answer the school's telephones, and a press release for the media. In case of a suicide, a fact-sheet concerning appropriate reporting of the death may be given to media representatives.

- Prepare a memorandum for teachers [see Appendix A] including the announcement, suggestions for being helpful to students, sign-in logs for counseling rooms, and forms to list the names of students referred for counseling or who may need monitoring for adverse reactions to the death.

- Identify, especially after a student suicide or other violent death, the deceased student's close friends and other friendship groups (e.g., sports teams or clubs). Make contact with these students and/or their parents.

- Decide if any schoolwide events (e.g., standardized testing or athletic events) need to be canceled or rescheduled.

- Designate rooms and school staff for counseling grieving students after the death is announced. Decide if community mental health professionals are needed.

- Brief those who will provide the counseling.

- Designate school personnel to monitor halls during class changes and restrooms throughout the day.

- Develop a plan of action for crowd control, emotional contagion, or disruptive behavior in the event these occur.

- Determine if parent meetings are advisable and work with parent organizations to schedule these.

- Notify the principal and/or counselor at other schools where close relatives (i.e., children, siblings, or parents) of the deceased are enrolled or employed.

_____3. The principal, or other designated staff member, checks with appropriate authorities (e.g., police department or coroner's office) concerning the facts (who, when, how, and where) of the death before the crisis task force meets, or as soon as possible. After a student suicide, it is advisable to secure parent permission before announcing the death. Do not characterize the death as a suicide until the cause of death is determined by the coroner's or medical examiner's office. (A coroner's decision is public information.)

_____4. The school principal contacts the deceased person's parents (or other next of kin) to offer condolences and to advise them of the school's planned response. (Note: Check local policy concerning flying a flag at half-mast following a death. Usually national and state flags are flown at half-mast only when approved by the appropriate governmental agency.

School staff need to be aware that any actions they take may set a precedent.)

_____5a. The school principal meets with all faculty and staff, including support and classified employees, to inform them of the death and planned response. At the principal's discretion, representatives of parent organizations or community leaders may be invited to this meeting. Each teacher receives an announcement about the death to be read at a designated time (e.g., the first period of the day). This announcement usually should not be made over the public address system.

Faculty and staff are provided the name and phone number of the district's approved media spokesperson (i.e., the principal, district crisis coordinator, or public information officer) to whom they should refer all media requests. Interviews with this spokesperson should be held away from the school campus and efforts made to keep reporters from interviewing or filming students at the school. The principal announces the time of subsequent faculty meetings (for example, at the close of the school day).

_____5b. If no faculty/staff meeting can be held, a telephone tree or a detailed memorandum to all faculty and staff is used to communicate the death. It is important that faculty members be fully informed before they meet with their students. Each telephone tree caller has accurate and identical information to relay.

_____6. At the faculty meeting, the school counselor (or other mental health professional) gives suggestions for assisting distraught students and explains the logistics of sending students for counseling. The principal requests that all teachers report to a designated place (e.g., the counseling office) during their planning or conference period to offer assistance.

_____ 7a. *Student death.* A counselor follows the deceased student's class schedule (in middle or high school) throughout the day or meets with the class of an elementary student to help classmates clarify their feelings and discuss concerns related to the death. A deceased student's desk should not be removed immediately.

_____7b. *Teacher death.* An experienced teacher on the campus (not a substitute teacher) meets the deceased teacher's class(es) the following day, and perhaps for several days. A school counselor or other mental health professional is present the first day to help students process their feelings about the death.

_____8. Volunteer counselors (from other schools or community agencies) sign in at a central location where they are provided name tags, maps of the school, and the teacher memorandum. Individuals who answer the school's telephones take information from callers who offer assistance. A designated staff person screens the information and approves all off campus volunteers.

_____9. A designated staff person removes personal effects of the deceased from classrooms and lockers. These items are screened and returned to the next of kin by a counselor, teacher, or the principal at a time convenient to the survivors. School staff follow local regulations concerning who may release suicide notes or written materials containing information about crimes or threats to others.

_____10. Near the end of the school day, the principal uses the public address system to call for a corporate moment of silence in memory of the deceased. The principal gives information about the funeral (or where this information will be available) and encourages students who need further assistance to contact a teacher or counselor.

_____11. The principal meets with faculty and staff at the end of the school day to assess the situation and receive feedback or suggestions concerning future actions. Counselors collect names of students who may need special help. This debriefing session also addresses the needs of the teachers and staff who are grieving or weary from assisting students. In some cases counseling is made available for teachers and staff.

_____12. The principal prepares a letter to parents, if deemed appropriate, or meets with concerned parent groups. (See Appendix A for a sample letter.)

_____13. Several days later, the crisis task force meets to consider the effectiveness of the response and to make notes for future crises. The group determines the appropriateness of any requests for memorials. (Note: In some circumstances, the task force or crisis team meets daily to reassess the situation until the crisis subsides.)

_____14. Several weeks later, and again on the anniversary of the event, the principal sends a follow-up memo to faculty and staff reminding them to be alert to students who may need special attention.

_____15. Several months after a death, a representative sample of students, faculty, and staff should be surveyed to determine what they believe worked well and what they wish had been done differently. Zinner (1985) discussed the importance of surveying individuals who were not close to the deceased ("secondary and tertiary group survivors") as well as those who had known the deceased well.[27]

V. Summary

A. Reactions That May Accompany Normal (Uncomplicated) Grief

    1. Physical Sensations

    2. Behaviors

    3. Feelings

    4. Cognitions

B. Bereavement Program for Students

    1. Facilities

2. Staff

3. Materials

4. Resources

5. Parental Notification and Permission

6. Procedures

    a. Meeting Place

    b. Understanding:

       Grief

       Shock

       Denial

       Bereavement Process/Journey

C. Determinants of Grief

1. Who the person was

2. The nature of the attachment

3. The mode of death

4. Historical antecedents

5. Personality variables

6. Social variables

D. Tasks of Grief

1. To accept the reality of the loss

2. To experience the pain of grief

3. To adjust to an environment in which the deceased is missing

4. To withdraw emotional energy and reinvest it in another relationship

E. Effective Bereavement Counseling

1. Effective counselors

Endnotes

[1] Alan D. Wolfelt, "Toward an Understanding of the 'Going Crazy Syndrome,'" *Thanatos* 17, no. 3 (fall 1992): 7-8.

[2] *Id.* at 7.

[3] *Id.* at 9.

[4] Reprinted with permission from *Pastoral Bereavement Counseling: A Training Program for Caregivers in Ministry to the Bereaved*, by Patrick M. Del Zoppo, Pys.D., C.A.S., page 42, ©1993 by Archdiocese of New York, Family Life/Respect Life Office. All rights reserved.

[5] Martha D. Oates, *Death in the School Community: A Handbook for Counselors, Teachers, and Administrators* (Virginia: American Counseling Association, 1993), 20.

[6] 20 USC 1232(h) (1995).

[7] 34 CFR 98.4(c)(1).

[8] No student can be required to submit to psychiatric or psychological examination, testing, or treatment in which the primary purpose is to reveal, among other information: mental and psychological problems potentially embarrassing to the student or his family; sexual behavior and attitudes; illegal, anti-social, self-incriminating, and demeaning behavior; critical appraisals of other individuals with whom respondents have close family relationships; and legally recognized privileged and analogous relationships, such as those of lawyers, physicians, and ministers. 20 USC 1232(h) (1995).

"Required" is not defined. It implies that it is not voluntary. Schools are to determine if a student is "required" to submit to a survey, analysis, or evaluation by making individual judgments in individual cases. If a complaint is made to the Department of Education, it will determine the situation on a case-by-case basis in light of all of the circumstances. 60 Fed. Reg. 44607.

[9] See "Reactions in the Normal Grief Experience" chart, *supra*.

[10] Patrick M. Del Zoppo, *To Be Lifted Up: The Journey from Grief to Healing* (New York: Archdiocese of New York, 1989), 6.

[11] *Id.* at 5-6; Del Zoppo, Pastoral Bereavement Counseling, *supra* note 4 at 45.

[12] J. William Worden, *Grief Counseling and Grief Therapy: A Handbook for the Mental Health Practitioner* (New York: Springer Publishing Co., 1982), 10, 13. Adapted with permission.

[13] *Id.* at 29-31.

[14] *Id.* at 10.

[15] *Id.* at 11-16.

[16] *Id.*

[17] Reprinted with permission from *Pastoral Bereavement Counseling A Training Program for Caregivers in Ministry to the Bereaved*, by Patrick M. Del Zoppo, Pys.D.,

C.A.S., p. 49, ©1993 by Archdiocese of New York, Family Life/Respect Life Office. All rights reserved.

[18] Therese A. Rando, *Grief, Dying, and Death: Clinical Interventions for Caregivers* (Illinois: Research Press Co., 1994) 82.

[19] James L. Greenstone and Sharon C. Leviton, *The Elements of Crisis Intervention* (California: Brooks/Cole, 1993) 80.

[20] Del Zoppo, *Pastoral Bereavement Counseling*, *supra* note 4, at 68-70.

[21] See the Grief Resolution Inventory in Appendix C.

[22] See Chapter 12, *infra*.

[23] Raymond Fox, *Elements of the Helping Process: A Guide for Clinicians* (New York: Haworth Press, 1993) 52-54.

[24] Lawrence Shulman, *The Skills of Helping: Individuals, Families, and Groups* (Illinois: Peacock Publishers, 1992) 86.

[25] Oates, *supra* note 5, at 19, 54, 59, 62, 72; Fox, *supra* note 23, at 52-54; Del Zoppo, *supra* note 4, at 68-71; Shulman, *supra* note 24, at 86.

[26] Oates, *supra* note 5, at 15-19.

[27] Reprinted from "Death in the School Community: A Handbook for Counselors, Teachers, and Administrators," ©1993, by Martha D. Oates, Ed.D., pp. 15-19. ACA (citations omitted). Reprinted with permission. (No further reproduction authorized without written permission of the American Counseling Association.)

CHAPTER 2

Bereavement Program for Parents

I. Introduction

In contemporary education, parental involvement in the school setting has become increasingly more prevalent, accepted, and, in many situations, quite beneficial.

As members of the "holistic" school community, parents will share in loss as will any other member of that group. It is therefore incumbent upon school officials to consider parents when establishing an in-house bereavement program and to provide for their inclusion. Grief reactions have the propensity to set into motion a multiplier — when the parents hurt, the children hurt, and, consequently, the caring school community hurts. Therefore, when there is parental bereavement, it is almost axiomatic that the school will be affected and should be concerned.

To better understand this interactive chain of events and the need for the school to consider parental bereavement as an integral part of any program that is undertaken, consider the following scenario:

When tragedy befalls a family, be it individual or extended, resulting in the death of a child, obviously the immediate impact is felt by the parents, siblings, and peers. Yet, despite the advantage of age and life experience, parents are frequently just as dazed, helpless, and vulnerable as any of the survivors. Not unlike younger grievers, parents also grope for answers and meaning, and flounder in their attempts to grasp and cope with the materialization of their own worst nightmare. Therefore, it is not only useful, but also essential, that provisions be made to help address and alleviate their pain. The focus of this chapter has this end in sight. It is an awesome task. However, one might consider the school pitifully remiss if it failed to respond when the proverbial "chips were down." Imagine the harmonic quality of the school day when parents, school aides, P.T.A. volunteers, and, perhaps, even faculty parents are caught up in unbridled grief. What happens when parents and staffers move about ineffectually, when absenteeism runs high, and when students are deprived of the guidance and support that they so desperately need?

27

When parents fall victim to the malaise and behaviors associated with their own untreated bereavement, children can be inadvertently left to their own grief behaviors, which are often fraught with pitfalls. It is precisely this possibility of parental "abandonment" at such a crucial time that can affect the children and their subsequent performance in the school environment. This potential reality underscores the intrinsic need for parental inclusion in the school-based bereavement program. Parents must "be there" for the children to cradle them, to understand their pain and their moods, to help them overcome survivor guilt, to prevent risk-taking behaviors or any of the many possible age-specific, negative grief reactions that are discussed in Chapters 5 and 6. To have a program without parental involvement would be like planting a tree without roots. How long would that tree last without nourishment, strength, and support?

II. Prescribed Bereavement Procedures

The procedures for a bereavement program for parents are not unlike those of a program for students as described in Chapter 1. The difference, if any, would be in the maturity level of the interventions and the hand-out materials.

Facilities should be provided in which counselors and parents can meet for individual and/or group counseling. A knowledgeable staff or "team" of certified bereavement counselors, clinical social workers, board of education bereavement personnel, and qualified guidance counselors should be available to provide individual or group intervention.

Appropriate materials, such as facial tissues, cups, water, and/or coffee, should be readily on hand as well as selected, appropriate reading materials and hand-out sheets. Bibliographies containing commercially prepared texts and theme-specific periodicals should be available for distribution. In some areas, community-based support groups may be available for the school community's needs.

The facilities and materials used in a bereavement program for parents are similar to those used in a program for students, again as outlined in Chapter 1. The intervention procedures to be followed will be mentioned later in this chapter and, in depth, in Chapter 3 and in Chapter 4. These procedures will include: (1) meeting in a quiet, comfortable, and uninterrupted setting; (2) empathic "tuning-in" while letting the mourners "tell their story"; (3) an explanation of the bereavement process as being a "journey" toward healing in which the path will wind its way through determinants of grief to be explored and tasks of grief to be mastered; (4) an explanation and exploration of the determinants of grief; and (5) an explanation and, hopefully, an accomplishment of the tasks of grief. These facilities and procedures in the hands of a skilled counselor can be a powerful force in guiding parents through such an incredibly difficult time.

III. Circumstances of Middle-Age Parents

As indicated earlier, all parents experience the same shock, disbelief, dazed helplessness, and despair following the death of a child. They all grope for answers and flounder in their incomprehension and inability to grasp and cope with such a devastating loss. However, a segment of these parents has an even greater problem. Not all parents of students are the same age. Older, middle-age parents may have their grief further complicated by pre-existing problems. Issues of age, health, economics, identity, and even their own immortality are brought into symbiotic conflict with mourning the death of a child. This particular parent group warrants closer analysis in order to understand the incredible stress under which it labors.

When one considers the array of developmental phases in the life cycle, it would seem apparent that each one would be unique with respect to specific stresses and stressors. Each phase would be a new experience and present new tasks to be learned and, hopefully, mastered.

How the middle-age stage of development within the life cycle and the death of a child impact each other is of primary importance if the older parents are to be effectively helped. With this knowledge, the skilled counselor will be able to perceive the individual's strengths and weaknesses and how assistance can be given to put these losses into a manageable perspective.

We will first consider an overview of the general characteristics, concerns, tasks, stresses, and stressors of the middle-age years prior to such a loss. This will be followed by a discussion of the extenuating factors that surround the death of a child and the necessary interventions designed to resolve the ensuing grief. It is important to note that the topics suggested in this chapter are ones about which volumes certainly can be written. The counselor is urged to use the citations wisely to increase his or her knowledge and skills.

The middle years of development in the life-cycle range are, approximately, from age 40 to age 65.[1] This stage is characterized by an assortment of varied and often conflicting emotional, physical, and psychological stresses and concerns.[2]

For many middle-age people, this stage in their lives is a happy and optimistic one. They begin to rejoice in a newfound freedom from the chores of raising children and begin to rediscover and refocus their mutual love. They are free to recapture their mutual interests and attentions with one another. Often, men will no longer feel the need to succeed in their careers and experience, instead, a renewed interest in reclaiming the intimate nuances of their "pre-children" marital life. Similarly, many career women may find this "post-children" period of their lives provides a renaissance of tempo and interest with respect to that career. Many middle-age couples find that this stage provides them, finally, with quality time for both independent and jointly shared activities, and time to form new friendships. Some will even pursue career changes.[3]

The above-scenario is, indeed, a wonderful point in parents' lives. They can eagerly look forward to expanding their horizons and circles of friends. If, however, they experience the death of a child, this "utopia" may change dramatically. The change is potentially true of all parental ages.

The death of a child is the embodiment of a parent's worst fears.[4] As such, the bereaved parents now become a constant reminder to others that this tragedy could befall them also. Grieving parents may find themselves subject to social avoidance or even ostracism, leading them to feel like "social lepers." The bereavement counselor must be attuned to this phenomenon because it can open up additional avenues of hurt caused by others' insensitivity. The bereaved parents may interpret this social rejection as a reinforcement of their own devalued self-esteem at not having been able to protect their deceased child.[5]

The astute bereavement counselor must confront this issue in addition to the normal protocol of bereavement counseling. A further treatment of the role and types of guilt will be discussed in Chapter 12. Other issues still remain.

As inviting as middle-age may sound, it is, however, fraught with its own pitfalls and setbacks. In many cases, it is not the expected "second honeymoon." Diminished physical capabilities begin to appear during the middle years. Hearing, reaction time, motor and sensory motor skills also are likely to decline.[6] Increased health problems in the forms of heart disease, respiratory ailments, and other cardiovascular complications are leading causes of death in this age group. Arthritis also begins to exact its toll during this life stage. Cancer, which claims lives at all ages, appears as the second-ranking cause of death in this age group — lung cancer in men and breast cancer in women.[7]

Menopause in women often is seen in an alternating light. Some women experience physical discomforts such as headaches, dizziness, palpitations, hot flashes, and vaginal dryness due to hormonal changes. These symptoms also may be accompanied by bouts of depression over the demise of reproductive ability, especially among those women who did not have children. Yet, in a significant number of other cases, some women experience a sense of relief and find sexual activity more pleasurable because they no longer need be concerned with pregnancy or contraception.[8]

It is important for the bereavement counselor to factor in parental health deficits when considering a treatment plan. Existing medical problems, such as the ones highlighted above, may, in fact, have to be considered as very real, additional losses for the bereaved parents. The counselor will have to break down or "partialize" these losses and deal with them individually and explore these issues with the bereaved parents and how they relate to their own grief resolution.

Not all problems affecting the middle years, however, are health related. Often, middle-age individuals are forced to overcome economic and financial obstacles, problems maintaining the "status quo," and subtle discrimination because of age. They may have to enact a realignment of family roles and responsibilities in order to establish a new equilibrium.[9]

It appears that individuals in the middle-age stage of the life cycle are often enveloped, if not overwhelmed, by a host of stage-specific problems. To this disturbing scenario the exigencies of life sometimes introduce what is possibly the most tragic and devastating of all human experiences — the death of a child. Arnaldo Pangrazzi encapsulates the trauma of this kind of loss so precisely: "When we lose a parent, we grieve over the loss of our past. When we lose a spouse, we grieve over the loss of our present. When we lose a child, we grieve over the loss of our future."[10]

Basically, the effective bereavement counselor must consider not only the parent(s), but also the attendant psychosocial and medical problems for this age group. Concurrent problems, left untreated, can complicate and delay normal grief resolution. The wise counselor may seek to refer some of these problems to other professionals for appropriate treatment. Several additional circumstances may inhibit grief resolution. "Disenfranchised grief" is a grief that is experienced when a loss is incurred yet can't be overtly mourned, acknowledged, or socially sanctioned.[11] Three factors contribute to this phenomenon. First, there is no recognition of the relationship to the deceased. This occurs when survivors may not be accorded the opportunity to grieve openly. A current example of this is found among "significant other" survivors of a homosexual relationship or the loss of a partner in an extramarital affair. Second, there is no recognition of the loss. Losses through abortion or perinatal death can result in significant grief reactions. In the school setting, this type of loss, within the framework of an illicit teenage pregnancy, can cause a student untold pain and grief complications. Finally, there is no recognition of the griever. Frequently, grievers toward the extreme ends of the age continuum are perceived as not having a significant comprehension of a loss experience. Elementary school children typically are seen as "bouncing right back." There is little inclusion of these children in the mourning process. The elderly and the mentally disadvantaged also may frequently fall into this grouping.[12]

IV. Extenuating Factors with the Death of a Child

Concern for the future is one of the considerations of middle-age people. The death of a child affects the equilibrium of the family and even the stability of the marriage itself.[13] Bereaved parents experience great difficulty in comforting each other due to their individual preoccupation with their own grief. This may cause stress in the marital relationship.[14] Each mate may tend to expect too much from the other while he or she is unable to give. Each one cannot realistically demand of the other while both are engulfed in identical pain. Parents should seek to work through their losses individually. The suggestion is gently given that bereaved parents can seek the aid of a professional counselor to share their pain and guide them empathically.[15] It is not uncommon for middle-age parents, owing to pre-existing crises, to be unable to overcome the loss of a child and even to have their marriages fail. With the death of a child, parents often experience various other secondary losses, "[t]hose losses that develop as a consequence of the death."[16] These losses require the counselor's attention. He or she must be able to help the parents identify their capacities and incapacities, as well as secondary losses, and guide them along the path to healing. It is appropriate, now, to consider some of these secondary losses.

The middle-age parent who may be concerned with present or future health conditions sees the loss of a future caregiver. He or she also sees the loss of the future in the loss of his or her own mortality. Parents' dreams, hopes, and aspirations for the future are buried with their child.[17] In addition, parts of themselves are lost as well. Middle-age parents, already concerned with problems of financial, emotional, and psychological security, are robbed of the companionship, closeness, and intimacy of the relationship they shared with their child. This loss can be likened to losing a vital organ necessary to sustain life. The ultimate loss is one of parental identity. The adult, on becoming a parent, takes on the identity of doing and providing for that child. This identity and its functions become basic elements of adulthood. It is no surprise, then, to see the parent greatly diminished by the loss of a child. Through death, the parents are abruptly stripped of their functional role. They experience a diminished sense of power and ability. They may feel violated and even exhibit some confusion and decreased self-esteem. The skilled bereavement counselor must be attuned to parental feelings of emptiness, insecurity, and disillusionment. He or she can help the parents by guiding them through the mourning and helping them to accomplish the necessary identity shift. Parents must be assisted to relinquish their former assumptions and beliefs concerning themselves and their capabilities as parents.[18]

The bereavement counselor also may direct parents to a bereavement support group that is focused on the loss of a child. These groups can provide hope and mutual support for parents and families as they adapt to the particular loss in their lives. Such groups are guided by experienced facilitators and can accompany the parents as they journey through grief toward healing.

Further complicating parental grief and the difficulty parents have grasping the loss of a child is that it is contrary to the natural order.[19] A child, at any age, should not die before the parent. When this does occur, it sometimes may be interpreted by the parent as a form of punishment for their own transgressions and/or failures,[20] leaving the parent to struggle with feelings of guilt and blame.

While much of death-related guilt is irrational and circumstantial, there are situations of "real guilt" based on "real culpability."[21] In the fictitious case of Bob one can see how these feelings can operate:

> Bob is in his mid-thirties, single, and is the last remaining child to live at home with his mother. One day, Bob went to a family picnic. Mother was not feeling well that day and had urged him to go without her. When Bob returned home, he found Mother on the floor, dead, from a heart attack. Bob experienced terrible guilt for having left her alone. He felt that if he had been there, he could have prevented her death. Although his doctor assured him that this was not the case, Bob felt that he had, in fact, killed her. Subsequent counseling focused on the fact that there was no real culpability and that Mother's death was purely unavoidable and circumstantial.

With irrational guilt, the bereavement counselor can be effective by pointing out that reality testing will often defuse this type of guilt because the guilt cannot be substantiated. Frequently, parents feel that they could have done more to help the child or even could have prevented the death. Realistically, in most cases, they will come to realize that they did all that they could have done. When there is "real culpability," the guilt is more difficult to treat and the wise counselor will defer to professional therapists for appropriate treatment.[22] While the role of guilt will be discussed further in Chapter 12, it would be useful at this point to consider some of the ramifications of parental guilt and thoughts of "punishment."

In addition to common parental feelings of helplessness, parents share feelings of having been personally culpable for their child's safety and welfare. When confronted with the death, parents may focus on irrational reasons as to why they "failed." Furthermore, when parents reflect on their relationship with their child and begin to compare their performance to some "ideal standard," feelings of guilt often can ensue. Also, having a child die before the parent does leaves the parent open to the added feelings of survivor guilt.[23]

Often tied into feelings of guilt is the perception that the death of one's child is, in essence, some form of punishment for failures that occurred earlier in the parent's life. This form of "moral guilt" is more prevalent among parents who are excessively scrupulous or whose religious beliefs may place emphasis on guilt, retribution, and atonement. Parents may view the death of their child as some form of punishment for having had an extramarital affair, or an abortion, or a pre-marriage pregnancy, for example. These feelings are not unusual and, while they may be irrationally tied to the parental loss, they should be addressed. Parents should be encouraged to confront these feelings, examine them, and seek professional help in their quest for self-forgiveness.[24]

When parents are faced with mitigating feelings of guilt, certain positive adaptive behaviors should be considered in an effort to develop effective coping mechanisms. After having confronted the existence of these haunting feelings, parents should seek to share them with others, while learning that feelings of guilt are normal and that it's OK to have them. Parents should be encouraged to focus their thoughts on the positive aspects of the experiences they shared with the deceased child, as well as the relationship they enjoyed. The bereavement counselor may suggest that parents remember the good things they did for the child during his or her lifetime. Finally, parents may wish to make this tragedy "count," to have something positive emerge from it. They can establish scholarships, work with other parents in bereavement groups, assist other children, or join social groups that seek to protect children. These activities, along with forgiveness, rational thinking, and using positive reinforcement, are viable means of coping with parental guilt feelings.[25]

V. Consideration of Determinants and Basics of Grief

After considering the variety of circumstances facing parents when they experience the loss of a child, the counselor, in order to be a true catalyst in the healing process, must be fully cognizant of this process and see it as a "journey" to be undertaken. It is a journey that will take the parents through a labyrinth of thought, reflection, and healing. The wise counselor knows that one must go through the grieving process, and not around it. One must be helped to confront the reality that this death has, indeed, occurred. One must experience the pain of the loss, the disillusionment, the confusion, and the myriad accompanying feelings. This is necessary, not only to manage the devastating emotional impact, but also to help transform thoughts of the deceased from piercing pain to a cherished memory.[26] But how is this done? Obviously, this must be done with great patience, empathic listening, and through a thorough consideration of the determinants and tasks of grief.

While these determinants and tasks will be seen in greater depth in Chapters 3 and 4, we will highlight their components here

To fully comprehend the extent of the loss it is necessary for the survivor to put into perspective just who the deceased was — Who in the life cycle has died? The nature of the attachment and the quality of the relationship must be explored. How the victim died will be an indicator of survivor grief as well as certain historical antecedents, for example, how the survivor resolved previous losses, his or her mental state, and existing life crises at the time of the death. The survivor's personality is also a determinant to be explored. Age, sex, the ability to express oneself, the ability to handle anxiety and stress are all important factors in one's ability to grieve normally.[27]

Finally, the counselor's ability to understand and relate to the social, ethnic, and religious background of the survivor may have a significant effect on the course of grief resolution. It is important for the counselor to be aware of customs, attitudes, beliefs, and rituals to avoid offending errors that could impede the grieving process.[28]

Once the determinants of grief have been sufficiently explored, the skilled counselor can personalize and tailor interventions in order to usher the survivor through the tasks to be accomplished for successful healing. These tasks must be accomplished for the survivor to reestablish equilibrium and complete the process of mourning.[29]

There are four basic tasks of grief to be accomplished.[30] The survivor must first "accept the reality of the loss." No progress can be made when one is in denial. Once the death is acknowledged the survivor can move on to the next task, which is "to experience the pain of the grief." One must be prepared to experience the pain of the grief and not try to avoid it. Avoidance would only be a negation of this task and would be counterproductive.

Once the survivor has accepted the reality of the loss and has experienced the pain of the grief, it is time "to adjust to an environment in which the deceased is missing." In order to do this, the mourner must determine just what is missing and may have to assume some, or all, of the roles played by the deceased. The successful adaptation of these roles can be pivotal in grief resolution.[31]

The final task to be accomplished is "to withdraw the emotional energy invested in this relationship and reinvest it in another." The mourner must realize the need to withdraw the emotional energy that was invested in the relationship with the deceased. He or she must learn to let go without guilt and to reinvest this energy in other relationships, indeed, in life itself.[32]

VI. Summary

A. Bereavement Program for Parents

1. Parents need bereavement programs as much as children do.

2. Parents also are at a loss for answers.

B. Bereavement Procedures

1. Facilities

2. Staff

3. Materials

4. Resources

5. Procedures

C. Circumstances of the Middle-Age Parent

1. Varied and sometimes conflicting emotional, physical, and psychological stresses

a. Positive factors

- Freedom from child-rearing responsibilities
- Re-focus love for each other
- Recapture intimacy of pre-children years
- New careers, interests, and friendships

b. Negative factors

- Decline in sensory and motor skills
- Increased health problems
- Socio-economic changes
- Security and status quo

D. Extenuating Factors with the Death of a Child

   1. Equilibrium of the family

   2. Stability of the marriage

   3. Loss of future caregiver(s)

   4. Loss of parental identity

   5. Loss of immortality

   6. Contrary to the natural order

E. Determinants of Grief

   1. Who the person was

   2. The nature of the attachment

   3. The mode of death

   4. Historical antecedents

   5. Personality variables

   6. Social variables

F. Tasks of Grief

   1. To accept the reality of the loss

   2. To experience the pain of grief

3. To adjust to an environment in which the deceased is missing

4. To withdraw emotional energy and reinvest it in another relationship

Endnotes

[1] Grace J. Craig, and Riva Specht, *Human Development: A Social Work Perspective* (New York: Prentice Hall 1987), 209; Carel B. Germain, *Human Behavior in the Social Environment* (New York: Columbia University Press, 1991), 395.

[2] Craig and Specht, *supra* note 1, at 209.

[3] Germain, *supra* note 1, at 396.

[4] Therese A. Rando, *How To Go On Living When Someone You Love Dies* (New York: Bantam Books, 1991), 169.

[5] *Id.*

[6] Craig and Specht, *supra* note 1, at 210.

[7] *Id.* at 211.

[8] *Id.* at 215; Germain, *supra* note 1, at 397-98.

[9] Germain, *supra* note 1, at 396.

[10] Arnaldo Pangrazzi, "Overcoming Grief: Ten Suggestions," *St. Anthony Messenger* (Reprint) (Jan. 1983): 2.

[11] Kenneth J. Doka, (ed.) *Disenfranchised Grief. Recognizing Hidden Sorrow* (San Francisco: The New Lexington Press, 1989), 4-6. Adapted with permission.

[12] *Id.*

[13] J. William Worden, *Grief Counseling and Grief Therapy: A Handbook for the Mental Health Practitioner* (New York: Springer Publishing Co., 1982), 100-101.

[14] Vanderlyn R. Pine, and Carolyn Brauer, "Parental Grief: A Synthesis of Theory, Research, and Intervention" in *Parental Loss of a Child*, ed. T. Rando (Illinois: Research Press Co., 1986), 70-71.

[15] *Id.*

[16] Therese A. Rando, (ed.) *Parental Loss of a Child* (Illinois: Research Press Co., 1986), 234.

[17] Ernest Becker, *The Denial of Death* (New York: The Free Press, 1973), 152-53.

[18] Therese A. Rando, *Treatment of Complicated Mourning* (Illinois: Research Press Co., 1993), 614-19.

[19] Rando, *supra* note 16, at 223.

[20] *Id.*

[21] Worden, *supra* note 13, at 42.

[22] *Id.*

[23] Margaret S. Miles, and Alice S. Demi, "Guilt in Bereaved Parents" in *Parental Loss of a Child*, ed. T. Rando (Illinois: Research Press Co., 1986), 100, 106.

[24] *Id.* at 106-07, 113-15.

[25] *Id.* at 113, 115-16.

[26] Worden, *supra* note 13, at 10, 13.

[27] *Id.* at 29-31.

[28] *Id.* at 31.

[29] *Id.* at 10.

[30] *Id.* at 11-16.

[31] John Bowlby, *Attachment and Loss: Loss, Sadness, and Depression* (Vol. 111) (New York: Basic Books, 1980), 139.

[32] Worden, *supra* note 13, at 11-16.

CHAPTER 3

Determinants of Grief

I. Introduction

Whenever a death occurs, whoever the deceased may be, certain factors must be questioned, examined, or considered. Once these have been adequately explored, the tasks involved in the successful resolution of that grief can begin. Each person will have his or her own form of grief reaction, and this must be taken into account. This idiosyncratic grief must be explored and understood in order to properly tailor the interventions to meet the needs of the particular individual(s).[1]

In advocating effective counsel to the bereaved, one researcher supports the empathic skills of the helper.[2] The counselor must be able to conceptualize the loss from the survivor's perspective and make every attempt to feel the pain that the loss has produced in each individual from the griever's "frame of reference." If the grief experience is viewed solely from the counselor's repertoire of experiences, the helping process will run the risk of being seriously compromised. To truly comprehend the extent of the loss event and the grief reaction, the counselor must be able to appreciate what that death meant to that person at that time.

II. Six Categories of Determinants

While it is difficult to predict the exact course of a person's idiosyncratic grief journey, it is possible to gauge the severity, intensity, and length (duration) of the survivor's grief experience by analyzing certain salient factors.[3] To accomplish this, the astute bereavement counselor will have to undertake an exploratory inventory of "determinants of grief."[4] These determinants encompass six strategic categories.

To begin the exploration, it is necessary to know just who the person was — who in the cycle of life has died; not just a name, but what he or she was all about.

To predict how someone will grieve, it is necessary to know something about the person being grieved for. One will grieve much differently over the death of a child than for the loss of a sibling. Like-

43

wise, the loss of one's grandfather will be grieved much differently than the death of a cousin or distant friend.[5] The loss of a person to whom the survivor had significant ties will result in the most intense and enduring reactions. This relationship will be a strong factor in many post-loss reactions.[6]

In addition to the survivor's relationship to the deceased, it is necessary to explore the nature of the attachment, some basic facts about its depth and strength. "It is almost axiomatic that the intensity of the grief is determined by the intensity of the love."[7] In addition, one must examine the security of the attachment. Was the survivor dependent on the deceased to validate his or her self-esteem and well-being? The extent of this security is a factor in the extent of the grief experience.

Finally, the degree of ambivalent feelings must be explored. In any given close relationship, there is bound to be both positive and negative feelings. Within a highly ambivalent setting, where these feelings coexist almost equally, there often will be strong manifestations of guilt and anger. Questions such as — "Did I do enough?" and resentment for being left behind, alone, is commonplace. These factors concerning the type of attachment that existed should be openly explored with the survivor.[8]

The mode of death, or how a person may have died, will be indicative of the survivor's grief. The suicide of a father will be felt to a different extent than the untimely death of a young mother; the natural death of a grandfather will be grieved differently than the accidental death of a young child. Additional dimensions associated with the mode of death include: Did it happen unexpectedly or was there sufficient warning? Did it happen close to home or, geographically, a distance away? At times, the circumstances accompanying a death may affect the survivor's ability to express anger or blame.[9]

Frequently, the survivor may view his present loss reactions as a repetition of behavior patterns already in place from past experiences and losses. It is difficult to conceptualize how difficult a person's grief journey will be without first considering some important historical antecedents. The counselor must explore information relative to how the survivor dealt with previous loss issues or events. Were these losses adequately resolved or is the griever bringing prior "problematic baggage" into the resolution of the present loss event? Is, perhaps, a prior mental illness (for example, depression) going to impede the grief resolution at hand? Life changes and transitions experienced by the survivor in the months prior to the death event also may be a determinant in the grief resolution process. If the resolution of difficult changes has been problematic, one can only question the ease of adjustment when confronted with the loss of a loved one.

Obviously, exploring the historical antecedents is an essential and important piece of psychosocial investigation. The results of this exploration can yield significant data that can provide the counselor with beneficial insights in his or her efforts to guide the bereaved through the difficulties of the grief process. However, more inquiry is needed.

A logical sequitur to the above explorations is a careful examination of personality variables. Through an awareness of these factors the bereavement counselor can get a basic grasp of a survivor's ability to grieve. Variables such as age, sex, one's ability to manage stress and anxiety, and inhibitions toward self-expression all provide meaningful insights for the concerned counselor. Once again, a prior mental history can have great importance. The griever who has a diagnosed personality disorder is particularly vulnerable to unpleasant loss reactions. Individuals classified with narcissistic and borderline personality disorders are particularly susceptible to this vulnerability.[10]

To complete the psychosocial nature of the determinants of grief, the effective bereavement counselor also must consider certain social variables. Even a casual glance at today's multicultural society will give the counselor an acute awareness of the many distinctly different religious, ethnic, and national influences that can come into play in the successful resolution of the grief process. Basically, knowledge of the survivor's background will do much to enhance the counselor's effectiveness and can tell much about the course that the survivor's grief will take. Each individual's unique background will dictate certain forms of behaviors and procedures. The skilled counselor would do well to be attuned to these differences, as they can provide useful insights for intervention. Customs or rituals, such as the Catholic anniversary Mass, the Jewish custom of unveiling the headstone or sitting Shivah, and the various protocols for wakes or services, are all important variables that impact the grieving process. Exploring each

45

person's distinct background will help the counselor adequately anticipate the griever's experience.

One final topic that should be considered in this discussion is the survivor who may obtain secondary gains through his grieving. At times a griever can extract gains from his or her individual social environment, such as extra consideration, pity, and sympathy, from an extended expression of grief. Significant gains may affect the length of the grieving.

However, protracted expressions of grief can become counterproductive and may even result in social alienation. Counselors should be aware of this type of griever, who often is called a "professional mourner." There may be other considerations involved that may necessitate an appropriate referral.[11]

The foregoing discussion of determinants of grief presents the bereavement counselor with a fairly comprehensive array of possible contingencies that can impact the survivor's grief process. It must be understood, however, that any given individual will have his or her own unique and personal psychosocial history. Consequently, the suggested exploration can yield any number of the factors mentioned.

III. Application of Determinants

In any comprehensive school bereavement program, counselors may be called on to assist one or more members in both single family and multiple family settings. Obviously, a significant amount of work will be needed to adequately serve these participants. To fully comprehend the importance of the determinants of grief and the information they can afford the counselor, we will examine the circumstances surrounding a death event in a sample family system. It is interesting to note the information that emerges.

> John is a 15-year-old high school sophomore. He is of Italian heritage and is the youngest of four children. His father, American-born, holds a doctorate and is a college professor. His mother, foreign-born, also is well educated, holding a master's degree.

> John has three siblings: the eldest brother, Tony, age 23, who has just died after a short illness; a brother Michael, age 17, who is a high school senior; and a

sister, Maria, age 21, who is completing college after a six-month hospitalization for a bipolar-affect disorder.

Tony was an exceptionally bright young man. He was an electrical engineer who was working on high-tech aerospace projects. He and Father shared a very special intellectual bond. Father is grieving this loss as as well.

Father is an erudite, scholarly man who is not overly demonstrative. He feels the loss of both a son and a brilliant mind, and chooses to experience his grief privately. Mother, on the other hand, is totally overwhelmed and is given to periods of vociferous lamentation. She is, for the most part, in an acute state of shock. She exhibits great anger toward the illness that "took him." Michael, like Mother, externalizes his pain and is quite vocal. This has been his behavior pattern throughout his life. Maria, while expressing appropriate levels of grief, shows no signs of regressive behavior and is not in need of professional intervention. John exhibits appropriate grief reactions and is the most accepting of Tony's death. Actually, it is John, who has occasionally assisted at a neighborhood funeral home, who has an inordinately mature orientation toward death and funerals. In fact, John leads the family in making the final preparations and selections.

The family is planning to observe the traditional Italian/Catholic, three-day wake, will have Masses said, and will observe a one-year period of mourning. Fortunately, the family has many caring relatives, friends, and professional colleagues to help them along the journey.[12]

It is of significant value for the bereavement counselor to take a closer look at the dynamics in operation in John's family. Within the framework of the determinants of grief, one can begin to accumulate pertinent data concerning this death event. The data presented in this vignette tells the counselor that the deceased was a brilliant son of professional parents as well as a brother to three younger siblings.

It is evident that Father and Mother are feeling the parental loss of a son. In addition, Father is mourning the loss of a brilliant mind and intellectual companion. The siblings are feeling the loss of a brother. John, the youngest, because of the age difference as well as his experience with the funeral home, seems to have distanced himself enough to view Tony's death more objectively than does the rest of the survivors. The family seems to be viewing the loss in the here and now. There are no indications that the parental "loss of future" is being considered at this point.

How Tony died is evident — a short-term, fatal illness. While Father is relatively quiet, Mother expresses great anger with the disease. There is, however, no anger shown toward medical personnel or the hospital.

At the time of Tony's death, there apparently was no other life crisis in operation for any of the family members, nor were there any unresolved issues from previous losses. For the siblings, this was their first crisis of an intimate nature. Father and Mother appear to be too consumed with their individual grief to consider previous losses or their resolutions. Fortunately, the extent of Maria's recovery from her illness prevented any relapse.

The death event in this vignette depicts how each family member is able to grieve as their personality allows. Father is quiet and pensive while Mother is "in a fog" and is given to outbursts of grief. Michael, too, is given to verbalization. However, as indicated earlier, this is how he customarily reacts to stressful events. John and Maria seem to maintain a more balanced affect. All in all, the three siblings appear to be coping fairly well.

The family is planning to observe traditional cultural and religious funerary rituals and procedures. The extended period of official mourning may, to an extent, affect the length of the grief process. Fortunately, the family appears to have a good support system, and one must wait to see if the grieving period will be unduly extended and, if so, for what reason(s).

Once the bereavement counselor realizes how much information can be generated by interviewing a single family system following a death event, he or she can get a better grasp of how much more can emerge in the course of a school-based bereavement program that will involve members of multiple families, each with their own unique psychosocial histories. The wealth and variety of data that is bound to emerge can aid the counselor in streamlining and tailoring appropriate interventions to meet the needs of the participants. The exploration of the variables discussed in this chapter are not only important, but are, indeed, at the very core of a sound and viable counseling program.

IV. Summary

    A. When a Death Occurs

        1. Certain factors must be considered

        2. Individual (idiosyncratic) grief reactions

        3. Tailor interventions to meet needs of participants

    B. Effective Counseling

        1. Empathic skill of counselor

        2. Conceptualize the loss

            a. Feel the pain from the survivor's point of view

        3. Understand what the death means to the survivor

        4. Predict the severity, intensity, and duration of grief

    C. Determinants of Grief

        1. The Deceased

            a. Who in the cycle of life died?

            b. What is the relationship to the deceased?

        2. The Attachment

            a. Intensity

            b. Security

            c. Degree of ambivalence

        3. The Mode of Death

            a. How the person died

     b. Timeliness of the death

     c. Geographic location

     d. Expressing anger/blame

  4. Historical Antecedents

     a. Resolution of previous losses

     b. Prior history of mental health (Depressive, or related disorders)

     c. Current life crisis (Previous changes and transitions)

  5. Personality Variables

     a. Age

     b. Gender

     c. Ability to manage stress and anxiety

     d. Ability/inhibitions with self-expression

     e. Prior mental history (Personality disorders)

  6. Social Variables

     a. Multicultural understanding of survivor's background

     b. How different people grieve

     c. Social, ethnic, and religious customs (rituals)

     d. Secondary gains

D. Case Study

  1. Value of Data Collection

Endnotes

[1] Therese A. Rando, *Grief, Dying, and Death: Clinical Interventions for Caregivers* (Illinois: Research Press Co., 1984), 43; J. William Worden, *Grief Counseling and Grief Therapy: A Handbook for the Mental Health Practitioner* (New York: Springer Publishing Co., 1982), 29.

[2] Rando, *supra* note 1, at 43.

[3] Patrick M. Del Zoppo, *To Be Lifted Up: The Journey From Grief to Healing* (New York: Archdiocese of New York, 1989), 11.

[4] Worden, *supra* note 1, at 29-31.

[5] *Id.* at 29.

[6] Del Zoppo, *supra* note 3, at 11.

[7] Worden, *supra* note 1, at 29-30.

[8] *Id.*

[9] John Bowlby, *Attachment and Loss: Loss, Sadness and Depression* (Vol. 111) (New York: Basic Books, 1980), 183.

[10] Worden, *supra* note 1, at 31.

[11] Adapted from "Determinants of Grief," *Grief Counseling and Grief Therapy: A Handbook for the Mental Health Practitioner.* J.W. Worden, Springer Publishing Co., Inc., New York. Used by permission.

[12] Adapted from "My First Crisis: How A Counselor Could Have Helped My Family," *Thanatos* 20 no. 2 (1995), A.J. Liotta, pp. 23-25. Used by permission.

CHAPTER 4

The Tasks of Grief

I. Introduction

Previous discussion has made it clear that grief is a response to a significant loss. However, this statement alone is insufficient to ease the pain. It is incapable of leading the survivor to a new, restructured life despite the absence of the loved one. To do this requires what is often referred to as "grief work." It is deliberate, it is painful, and it *is* work. Yet, it is the journey the griever must take to facilitate a successful resolution. The process has been described as "the intentional work engaged in by a person who has experienced a loss."[1] This work should emerge as a natural outgrowth of the exploration of the determinants of grief outlined in Chapter 3.

II. The Four Tasks

Once the determinants have been explored and clarified, personalized and tailored intervention can begin to accomplish what one researcher identifies as "the four tasks of mourning"[2] (referred to here as "tasks of grief"). Eventually, through the accomplishment of these tasks, the survivor will be better able to cope with his or her loss and to experience a measure of personal growth.

The first step on this "leg" of the journey is for the survivor to *accept the reality of the loss*. When death does occur, even when it is not unexpected, there is always a feeling that it didn't happen, that perhaps it was just a bad dream. This failure to accept, or denial of, the loss is not uncommon. However, the manifestation of the denial can traverse the continuum from a simple distortion of reality to the realm of delusion. One may keep the deceased's room just as it was for a short while; this is not unusual. Significant denial occurs if one were to continually lay out the deceased's clothing on a daily basis. The astute counselor must be constantly attuned to significant symptoms of denial and must be prepared to make an appropriate referral to a professional therapist.

A primary task of grief intervention is to help the survivor confront the reality that the death has, indeed, occurred; the deceased is gone and is not going to return. The griever does not have to and will not like it, but must be able to acknowledge the fact of death.

Grieving is a time to recognize and confront denial, to increase the emotional and intellectual awareness of the reality of the loss, and to consider and accept the life differences that have been affected by this death.[3]

Once the acceptance has begun, the survivor can begin to approach the next step, *to experience the pain of grief*. It is almost impossible to lose someone of significant attachment and not experience the pain of loss. Grief hurts; it is painful. "The bereaved cry for the lost object, yearn to repossess it, protest its absence."[4]

Although unpleasant, the pain cannot and must not be avoided. One must explore the loss and name the pain. One must go through the grief, and not around it, in order to grow. Once the feelings of pain have been identified and expressed, then they can be appropriately resolved, for example, anger can be expressed and targeted properly; guilt can be explored and repented if necessary.

Some people will travel to "forget" the pain. Others will avoid painful thoughts and seek only to idealize the deceased. Pleasant thoughts can buffer the painful ones. Whatever the case, survivors must be allowed to indulge in and experience the pain, knowing that it will not last forever. A failure to do so, avoidance, is not only a negation of this task, but can serve to prolong the grieving process and may even precipitate maladaptive behaviors.

One of the most difficult, yet most significant, of the tasks of grief is to *adjust to an environment in which the deceased is missing*. This is difficult to accomplish because in all the turmoil surrounding the loss, the survivor has to determine just what is missing. What makes it difficult is that, in addition to the actual loss of the deceased, the survivor frequently may not fully realize the extent and number of roles that the person actually played in life. This realization often does not fully emerge until after the loved one has died and the survivor finds himself or herself greatly diminished and overwhelmed. The pain of loss may leave one feeling "emotionally incomplete."[5]

In analyzing the attachment to the deceased, four key elements can be identified as factors in the relationship that anyone may have with a loved one: "safety, security, recognition and response."[6] These are the losses and roles that the survivor must identify. One must consider if the deceased played the role of, for example, protector, listener, sexual partner, friend, confidant, or family accountant. What is missing and what does one do now? This is the heart of the "going crazy syndrome"[7] that was discussed in Chapter 1.

Once the survivor has successfully identified the losses that accompany the death, he or she must move toward adjusting to the new life situation without the deceased and devoid of all the identified roles that person played. Not infrequently, a resentment emerges because the survivor is confronted with assuming some of these roles for himself. Sometimes, the acquisition of new skills may be necessary to perform certain roles. The author is reminded of a middle-age participant in a bereavement support group who was grieving the loss of his wife. The man was describing his loss and the facts surrounding the death event when, at a very poignant moment, he just broke down and blurted out, "It's not fair, she left all this for me to do." Perhaps it was unfair, yet his wife's death did leave him with things (roles) "to do." It is precisely this adaptation to new skills that will usher in the adjustment to the new environment without the deceased.

This task must not be avoided or ignored. To do so, would be to encourage helplessness and would deprive the survivor of the necessary coping skills essential for this adjustment and grief resolution in general. Part of this adjustment will focus on adapting to some of the secondary losses mentioned in Chapter 2. The accomplishment of this task is viewed by one researcher as a turning point in grief resolution.[8]

The final task in the resolution of grief is to *withdraw emotional energy and reinvest it in another relationship*. The survivor must now begin to withdraw all of the emotional energy (decathexis) that was invested in the relationship with the deceased in order to reinvest this energy in another relationship or, perhaps, even in life itself. The difficult part of this task is that sometimes people are reluctant to do this for fear of a false sense of disloyalty to the deceased. They may fear that the emotional withdrawal is, in fact, an act of dishonoring the deceased.

To the contrary, many researchers strongly suggest that this decathexis is absolutely essential to the successful resolution of the loss.[9] It is, in essence, to put the memory of the loved one into perspective while creating a cherished memory and to have the regained

55

emotional energy available to invest part of oneself (cathexis), once again, in a new relationship.

The disloyalty concept is refuted by researchers who indicate that the altered relationship will still exist in the survivor's mind and heart.[10] Yet, "[t]he energy that previously went into keeping the relationship with the deceased alive now must be channeled elsewhere, where it can be returned."[11] Feelings of guilt may hinder the accomplishment of this task by making the survivor hold on to past attendants that can impede the formation of new ones. The griever must learn to let go, without guilt, and to reinvest in life. How can this be done? The counselor must be aware that the process is painful, yet possible.

Patrick Del Zoppo addresses this point with a particularly keen insight. He explains how each contact with the loved one had been an investment of emotional energy. The decathexis can be effected by reviewing and reliving the total "repertoire" of the attachment. (The reader may wish to review the Determinants of Grief in the preceding chapter.) The telling and retelling of stories is the vehicle through which the bond can be felt and, eventually, let go. As these bonds are loosened, they become internalized as images and memories, paving the way for remembering without pain. Slowly, the regained energy becomes available for reinvestment in new relationships. The survivor will be able to "get on with life," heralding the completion of the painful grief journey.[12]

When the mourning process is actually finished is difficult to determine. To provide any given timeline for grief resolution would be misleading and could create unrealistic expectations and possibly disappointment. A generalized point of completion may be when the survivor is able to share pleasant thoughts of the loved one without the wrenching pain, while recathecting in a restructured life.[13]

III. Application of Tasks

While the case vignette concerning John's family, presented in Chapter 3, produced valuable information for the bereavement counselor, it dealt with the here and now of Tony's death and the impact it had on the family system at that time. However, given the information generated and the role of the tasks of grief, it is fair to say that some meaningful interventions can be planned to help this family through their grief journey. The astute counselor may wish to entertain the following suggestions:

1. Neither denial nor the realization of the finality of Tony's death appear to be a significant problem at this point. What is of concern is Mother's initial inability to accept the loss. At this point, she realizes that Tony will not return. She must be given the time and opportunity to vent her feelings as best she can. The remaining members of the family appear to have begun to accept the loss with less trauma. Yet, given the nature of the attachment between mother and child, with all the considerations discussed in Chapter 2, the counselor should easily grasp the dynamics of her loss. For now, comfort and empathic listening would seem most appropriate.

2. While Mother has no difficulty with expression and with feeling the pain, Father and the rest of the family should be encouraged to verbalize more. Father's silent involvement in his work may be an appropriate coping mechanism for him, or it may be an unproductive avoidance maneuver. This merits further exploration. Maria, on the other hand, given her psychiatric history, should be gently encouraged to express her feelings. The nonprofessional counselor is advised to tread gently with her, and to be on the alert for any signs of deterioration in her mood that would require an immediate referral for professional intervention. John and Michael do not appear to be exhibiting any extraordinary reactions that would merit immediate concern. Verbalization and expression of feeling would appear to be adequate at this point.

3. The entire family should become involved in the dynamics of task number three. Each member should be encouraged to "name the pain," to identify what is missing, and to express how this loss impacts their individual lives. As each role that Tony played is discussed, family members should be encouraged to acquire any necessary skills that he or she feels would help to fill the void of this role loss. This is difficult in that not all roles can be filled. The role of heir and future bearer of grandchildren, for example, cannot be filled by skills acquisi-

tion. However, the equilibrium or balance of the family may be renegotiated so that this role may be reassigned to the next oldest child. The crucial point is that each family member must do what is necessary to adjust to the new environment without Tony. This is essential for the grief process to be successfully resolved.

4. Once the family has "turned the corner" in their grief process and begins to adjust to family life without Tony, the final task remains for them to decathect their invested energies from their relationship with him. This will not be easy for this family. The Italian culture places great importance on respect, family, and honoring the memory of the deceased. (This in no way means that other cultures do not have the same values, it is just that this is a factor in this particular case history.) The bereavement counselor will have to use skill and sensitivity in encouraging decathexis in this case. In this family system, the reliving and retelling of stories and experiences is strongly recommended. Mother and Michael appear to be well suited for this. Father, Maria, and, to a lesser degree John, may need some encouragement to do so. This reliving and retelling will help family members internalize the memory of the deceased son and brother, and can foster the loosening of bonds which, in turn, can lead to the reinvestment of energies in other areas and relationships. Once accomplished, the journey from pain to healing will approach completion.

One does not have to be a professional therapist to comprehend the enormous impact that the tasks of grief have on the direction, quality, and efficiency of grief resolution. While the determinants of grief focus on the "Who," "What," and "Why," the tasks of grief focus on the "How" of grief resolution. Taken separately, it would leave an incomplete counseling program with questionable results. Yet, incorporated, in order, into a bereavement support program would produce interventions of significant value that can nurture the healing process.

Ultimately, the counselor will be dealing with "broken" human beings who will display a host of varying complexities: experiences, fears, feelings, anxieties, backgrounds, beliefs. In such an atmosphere, the bereavement counselor will find that the determinants and tasks of grief will provide a valuable framework for establishing meaningful interventions as well as functional and successful grief work.

As indicated earlier, the school-based bereavement counselor will find this vignette in multiples. The tasks are the same, regardless of the number of participants. The counselor must help the participants to sort things out, both individually and collectively, in an effort to ease their pain and help them to resolve their grief.

IV. Summary

A. Grief Work

1. Necessity

2. Painful

3. Facilitates grief resolution

B. Tasks of Grief

1. To accept the reality of the loss

a. Modes of denial

b. "Risk" of denial

c. Realize the finality of death

d. Confronting denial

2. To experience the pain of grief

a. Realize that grief hurts

b. Resisting the loss

c. Name the pain

d. Begin resolution of anger and guilt

e. Avoidance prolongs grief

3. To adjust to an environment in which the deceased is missing

a. "Going crazy syndrome"

Turmoil surrounding loss

   Feelings of being overwhelmed and diminished

  b. Analyze the attachment

   Determine what is missing

   Identify "roles" that are lost

  c. Adjustment to new life situation without deceased

   Acquisition of new skills

   Resentment at loss of roles played by deceased

   Danger of avoidance

  d. Adapting to secondary losses

  e. Turning point in grief resolution

4. To withdraw emotional energy and reinvest it in another relationship

  a. Decathexis

  b. Reluctance to decathect

   Fear of disloyalty/dishonor to deceased

  c. Decathexis essential to successful loss resolution

   Put memory of deceased into perspective

   Create a cherished memory

   Re-channel energy where it can be returned

   Learn to "let go"

C. When Mourning Is Completed

 1. No set time limit

 2. Ability to share thoughts of deceased without pain

 3. When recathecting in a restructured life

D. Use of Case Vignette

 1. Begin to implement tasks of grief

Endnotes

[1] Patrick M. Del Zoppo, *To Be Lifted Up: The Journey From Grief to Healing* (New York: Archdiocese of New York, 1989), 14.

[2] William J. Worden, *Grief Counseling and Grief Therapy: A Handbook for the Mental Health Practitioner* (New York: Springer Publishing Co., Inc. 1982), 11-16.

[3] Patrick M. Del Zoppo, *Pastoral Bereavement Counseling: A Training Program for Caregivers in Ministry to the Bereaved* (New York: Archdiocese of New York, 1993), 45.

[4] *Id.* at 45.

[5] John W. James, and Frank Cherry, *The Grief Recovery Handbook A Step by Step Program for Moving Beyond Loss* (New York: Harper and Row, 1988), 103-04.

[6] Del Zoppo, *supra* note 1, at 11.

[7] Alan D. Wolfelt, 'Toward an Understanding of the 'Going Crazy Syndrome,'" *Thanatos* 17, No. 3 (1992), 6-9.

[8] John Bowlby, *Attachment and Loss: Loss, Sadness, and Depression* (vol. 11) (New York: Basic Books, 1980), 139.

[9] Del Zoppo, *supra* note 3, at 46; Worden, *supra* note 2, at 15-16; Therese A. Rando, *Grief, Dying, and Death: Clinical Interventions for Caregivers* (Illinois: Research Press Co., 1984), 77.

[10] Rando, *supra* note 9, at 19.

[11] *Id.*

[12] Del Zoppo, *supra* note 1, at 16-17.

[13] Discussion of the tasks of grieving is adapted from *The Four Tasks of Mourning, Grief Counseling and Grief Therapy: A Handbook for the Mental Health Practitioner.* J.W. Worden, Springer Publishing Co. Inc., New York. Adapted with permission.

CHAPTER 5

When Children Grieve

I. Introduction

Dealing with the topic of child bereavement warrants an admonition of great caution. The understanding of the circumstances of the death event, the actual meaning of death, itself, and the impact of the loss on the life of the survivor is not nearly as focused and conceptualized as it is for the older griever. School officials must exercise caution and good judgment before attempting to implement a bereavement program for the younger survivors of loss. The nature of the many variables that will be discussed in this chapter, as well as the necessity for child specialists who are competent to effectively do this kind of counseling, require school officials to make a sensitive judgment call as to when and how this kind of program can be effectively carried out in a school-based setting. The intent of this chapter is to provide the stages, variables, and considerations that are necessary components of such a program.

One problem that school officials will encounter is determining just how much a child comprehends of death and how capable he or she is of mourning at any given age. Since the young, school-age child is going through the formative stages of life, the answer to this question will vary from child to child.

When the counselor considers the topic of child bereavement, a significant dichotomy becomes immediately evident. On the one hand is the age grouping that has acquired the cognitive and conceptual skills necessary to enable the children to grasp the dynamics of the "adult" concept of death (its finality, irreversibility, and the awareness of one's own immortality). On the other hand is the younger grouping of children who have not yet developed the capacity to conceptualize this adult understanding of death, and who cannot assign meaning to their distress or adequately verbalize their feelings. The question, of course, is what is the pivotal age at which this transition or skills acquisition is considered to have been accomplished?

The experts disagree on children's ability to mourn and sustain the pain of the object loss.[1] Some place the acquisition of this ability

63

between the ages of 8 and 10 years.[2] At these ages most children should be able to conceptualize the more mature concept of death, which comprises its permanence, irreversibility, universality, and inevitability, coupled with an understanding that death includes a total cessation of physical (bodily) functioning.

II. Developmental Variables

While volumes have been written concerning the psychology of infancy through pre-school years, the scope of this work requires a specific focus on the grief experience(s) of school-age children. With this mandate, it is appropriate to begin with a consideration of the variables that impact school-age first-graders.

The first-grade child, usually around age 6, finds himself or herself emerging from a phase of development in which there was little cognitive comprehension of death, with no recognition that it is irreversible. Death may have been considered as a departure or as something gradual, or even as being temporary. There was no concept of death entailing a total cessation of physical life functions. The child may have reacted with anger at the deceased for abandonment or desertion.[3]

When the child attains ages 5 through 8, he or she begins a progression toward the conceptualization of the causality of death and the developing capacity for guilt. There may exist a fear that some unkind, hostile, or "magical" thinking may have caused or contributed to the death.[4] There also is a tendency to personify death; it becomes like a person and can be referred to as one. Death can be thought to carry off a person.[5]

This age population is subject to several significant considerations. While children in this age group are beginning to have a cognitive awareness of death and its subsequent ramifications, there are certain vulnerabilities. Despite their increased understanding of death, the children have few coping skills in place to adequately handle grief.[6] It is important to bear in mind that, at this age, children's emotions and reactions to grief are not yet comparable to those of adults. Consequently, given their lack of experience and their still emerging (developing) personality, children can easily fall prey to misconceptions and confusion and, thus, can fail to grieve their loss.[7]

Children may exhibit sadness, denial, depression, guilt, and episodic crying. Of these possibilities, children's usual first line of defense is denial.[8] They are most apt to react as though nothing at all had occurred. Children tend to conceal their feelings and "fear exposure" and "loss of control." If and when they should feel the need to cry and express their emotions, they do so privately. While children may appear not to care or be noticeably affected, covertly they really need support and encouragement to grieve. They need someone to assure them that crying and sadness are appropriate, that it is okay to grieve. The child needs reassurance from patient, caring adults who can listen to them, validate their feelings, and encourage them.[9]

When the child attains ages 8 through 12, he or she begins to develop a more adult-like conceptualization of what death is. The older child begins to get a sense of his or her own mortality, the possibility of his or her own death, and the irreversible nature of the death event. The child gains the awareness that all physical (bodily) activity ceases. One can no longer see, taste, or feel. Death is universal in nature and eventually, inevitably, comes to everyone.[10]

Interestingly, among older children, if the death event is sudden, fright can be added to the previously mentioned list of reactions along with increased denial. The fragility of the older child's emerging independence can produce feelings of anxiety and anger. This anger may be masked in a cloak of irritability and frequently can go undetected. The child may be misdiagnosed as having some form of behavior problem. Children in this age group still may have difficulty in accepting death as a final event and can react inappropriately.[11]

One of the "dangers" of childhood grief is that often adults, with all noble intentions, attempt to shield children from their loss and try to lessen their pain. This type of insulation should be avoided. In addition to depriving the grief-stricken child of the much needed guidance and support of friendly adults, such misguided protection can actually set the stage for future life problems and even undesirable pathology.[12]

III. Basic Needs for Grief Resolution

The needs of the bereaved child must be carefully met in order to foster successful grief resolution and to avoid the pitfalls of unresolved or complicated grief. Just what, however, are these needs?

65

What can the astute bereavement counselor do, or provide, for these children? Reviews of the various age-specific developmental skills and grief responses available to bereaved children indicate at least five basic needs that should be provided to foster successful grief resolution.

First, children need adult assistance and a logical explanation of the nature of death. Inasmuch as children tend to express grief in behavioral terms, they need supportive adults to guide them in their struggle to effectively verbalize their feelings to use language, rather than behavior, as their vehicle of expression. Children need adults to discuss death with them rather than conceal it. They rely on adults "to help them begin to understand and grasp the grieving process."[13] Children need adult assurances that they will be all right. They need to be assured of the continued "safety, security, recognition, and response" discussed in Chapter 4.

Second, children need adult assistance to help them to accomplish the same tasks of mourning (see Chapter 4) that older people have to struggle with. This is a slow process. Children do not have a high threshold for pain. They must deal with their loss, and subsequent pain, in small doses.

Third, children may need assistance to keep their memory of the deceased alive, as their memory ability may be inadequate. Pictures, momentos, dates, and the assurance of the love the deceased had for them will all play a significant role in meeting this need for children.

Fourth, children will have to continue living with the absence of the loved one. Significant occasions will prompt memories of the deceased. Children will need assistance to decathect, to tell and retell stories (see Chapter 4) in order to internalize the images and memories of their lost loved one and ease the journey from pain to cherished memory.

Fifth, if the loss involves the death of a parent of a young child, there may be a need for a surrogate of the same sex to help the child identify with adults of that sex and determine what they are like. Preadolescents often may make their own surrogate selection. Frequently, the surrogate may be a teacher, an acquaintance, or an adult relative.[14]

IV. Guidelines for Intervention

Obviously, when children grieve it is a fragile journey for them. Their grief must be understood and guided carefully and skillfully. Without trained counselors and proper interventions for grief resolution, childhood grief may have the potential to lead to pathological disorders in the adult years. Some of the potential problems that counselors may observe during childhood grief are: sleep disturbances, depression, changes in appetite or habits, anger, sadness, episodic crying, psychosomatic and adjustment problems, separation anxiety, and guilt. These reactions are not unlike those experienced by grieving adults (see Chapter 1). Remember, however, that these are only possible consequences; there is no reason to believe that childhood bereavement must necessarily lead to any type of dysfunction.[15]

If the grieving child receives proper intervention services, the prognosis should be good for normal resolution of grief, devoid of significant dysfunction(s). The child would be happier, more secure, and better equipped to resolve future losses and other traumatic events. In adult life, the individual's ability to handle future losses may be affected by the degree to which previous losses have been resolved.[16] The adult concept of death has its formative roots in childhood.[17]

To provide the appropriate interventions for bereaved children, one need only probe the realm of crisis intervention for assistance. Death, at any age, produces a crisis for the survivor(s). Children, however, may tend to be more at risk than adults due to the many developmental variables previously discussed, their limited repertoire of experiences, and their frequent use of denial as a coping mechanism. Crisis has been defined as "a perception of an event or situation as an intolerable difficulty that exceeds the resources and coping mechanisms of the person."[18] Unrelieved, crisis potentially can produce dysfunction in the cognitive, behavioral, and affective domains.[19] This is not inconsistent with previously mentioned potential reactions that may befall the bereaved child.

A. Play Therapy

The medium for bereavement intervention with children should be consistent with that of any other given crisis for this age group — intervention through play therapy. This modality offers children the opportunity to work through their distress via an assortment of creative and expressive media.[20] Through play therapy, the child can express feelings that are too painful to convey verbally in a symbolic fashion.[21] While the "substance," the needs and tasks to be accomplished, has been clearly delineated, it is the "vehicle" of intervention that must now by determined. One researcher underscores the wisdom of using play as an intervention mode, stating that "[p]lay therapy is an appropriate treatment modality through late latency, with the likelihood that the balance between verbal and play interactions will shift gradually through the years."[22] This suggests that verbalization will most likely improve as the child advances in age.

The use of play therapy is virtually a necessity when counseling children since children are not prone to benefit from a lecturing modality. They will benefit more from strategies that tend to incorporate "concrete, tactile, enactment, and model observation modes."[23] Several appropriate, child-centered modalities are offered here for the reader's consideration.

1. The Use of Puppets

Children can benefit greatly through the use of puppet play. They can use a broad spectrum of their abilities to communicate and convey feelings. They can use identification, projection, and displacement as means of releasing their emotions. Through puppetry, children can safely act, touch, talk, and share as they develop constructive coping mechanisms. Fantasy and symbolic play are creative, therapeutic tools, and potential for success depends largely on the skill, imagination, and encouragement of the counselor.[24]

2. The Use of Music

Music therapy can be useful in effecting positive behavioral changes as well as enhanced self-expression. This modality is best used in a group setting in which children can be encouraged to share feelings safely in an atmosphere of mutual support. One of the therapeutic goals of this modality is to help children express their death-related fears and issues. Initially, familiar, playful music is used to foster introductions and a sense of security. Concepts and issues related to death are explored and explanations are given at appropriate age-specific levels of comprehension. The main thrust is to have the children create their own song(s) about the deceased loved one. These songs ultimately can be sung to their parents, who can continue the discussion further. Music therapy is used to effectively validate children's feelings of grief and help them gain positive insights from such a negative experience.[25]

3. The Use of Artwork

The use of artwork affords children a broad spectrum of expression that goes beyond the limitations of verbal communication. From simple scribblings to well-defined caricatures, the child is free to express what cannot be adequately verbalized. The variety and types of currently available molding materials provide the added benefit of letting the child safely express feelings of hostility without danger or fear. In addition, individual projects can be incorporated sequentially to create stories. Thus, a more global therapeutic experience is possible.[26]

4. The Use of Storytelling

Storytelling allows children to exercise their imaginative abilities in grief resolution. With this modality, children can be asked to tell a story about their experiences and reactions. The skilled therapist can then adapt the story while modeling more appropriate coping mechanisms to resolve conflict(s). This technique can be enhanced by having the child review a recording or videotape of himself or herself telling the story. The therapist can use selected portions of the story for diagnostic and information-gathering purposes.[27] An added advantage to this therapeutic approach is that stories can be retold and relived in an effort to internalize images and memories and loosen bonds (see Chapter 4).

5. Use of Sand Play

Sand play is a creative, therapeutic mode in which children are free to participate without the restrictions of verbal or graphic expression. They can be "more prone toward creative self-expression."[28] Sand is considered to be a familiar, non-threatening means of expression.[29]

The benefits of play therapy "are limited only by the imagination and creativity of the child and therapist."[30] The assortment of media that can be used in play therapy is limitless. Therapists are constantly using new and innovative techniques. Additional areas to be explored are board games, photography, and gardening.[31]

B. Key Elements of Intervention

As indicated earlier, many aspects of adult bereavement intervention are equally valid in counseling children when put into the appropriate age-specific context. However, certain key elements can be woven into any of the child-centered approaches that have been mentioned.

- Be open and honest in discussing facts about death. It should not be a matter of concealment. Conversations and specific interventions should be accomplished at appropriate levels of comprehension.

- It is important that the child be given permission to mourn. The child should be made to feel secure and have his or her feelings validated.

- A counselor can be a role model for grief expression. Crying and expressing grief appropriately is perfectly acceptable.

- As indicated earlier, children do not evidence their grief constantly. A child's covert feelings are not always revealed by overt reactions.

- A significant amount of childhood bereavement reactions can be addressed through multifaceted play therapy

- The counselor can enhance the child's feeling of security, and help him or her to identify the many confusing feelings and how to express them appropriately. The more these concerns can be treated in an open and honest fashion, the greater the child's success in resolving the loss.

- A child who is confronted with a sudden death event will probably require additional help to retrieve some of the security lost by the death.[32]

V. Summary

A. Exercise Caution and Good Judgment

1. When and how to implement children's bereavement program

2. Necessity for child specialists

B. Different Age Groupings

    1. Pre-school

        a. Little cognitive comprehension of death

        b. No recognition of irreversibility of death

        c. Death seen as gradual or temporary

        d. No concept of finality, cessation of bodily functioning

    2. Ages 5 through 8

        a. Progression toward conceptualization of causality of death

        b. Developing capacity for guilt and denial

        c. Magical thinking

        d. Personification of death

        e. Few coping skills in place to handle grief

        f. Episodic displays of grief

    3. Ages 8 through 12

        a. More adult-like conceptualization of death

        b. Sense of one's own mortality

        c. Recognition of irreversibility of death

        d. Awareness of inevitability, universality, and finality of death

        e. Issue of sudden death:

          Fright

          Anxiety

Anger

Behavioral Problems

C. Needs of Children

  1. Logical explanation of death

  2. No concealment

  3. Adult support to verbalize feelings

  4. Adult assurances to accomplish tasks of mourning

  5. Assistance to keep memories alive

  6. To continue living with the absence of the deceased

  7. Possible need for same-sex surrogate

D. Interventions

  1. Crisis intervention strategies for children

  2. Play therapy

    a. Use of puppets

    b. Use of music

    c. Use of artwork

    d. Use of storytelling

    e. Use of sand play

    f. Additional modalities of play therapy

E. Key Elements to Be Considered

  1. Honesty

  2. Permission to mourn

  3. Appropriate expressions of grief

  4. Covert feelings versus overt behavior

  5. Multifaceted play therapy

  6. Retrieving sense of security

Endnotes

[1] Barbara Saravay, "Short-Term Play Therapy with Two Preschool Brothers Following Sudden Paternal Death," in *Play Therapy with Children in Crisis* ed. N.B. Webb (New York: The Guilford Press, 1991), 177.

[2] Maria Nagy, "The Child's View of Death," in *The Meaning of Death*, ed. H. Feifel, (New York: McGraw-Hill, 1959), 81, 96-97. (original work published 1948.); Robin F. Goodman, "Diagnosis of Childhood Cancer," in *Play Therapy with Children in Crisis*, ed. N.B. Webb (New York: The Guilford Press, 1991), 313; Patrick M. Del Zoppo, *Pastoral Bereavement Counseling. A Training Program for Caregivers in Ministry to the Bereaved* (New York: Archdiocese of New York, 1993), 55.

[3] Nagy, *supra* note 2, at 80-81; Therese A. Rando, *Grief, Dying, and Death: Clinical Interventions for Caregivers* (Illinois: Research Press Co., 1984), 159.

[4] Rando, *supra* note 3, at 160; Saraway, *supra* note 1, at 178; Robert Kastenbaum, *The Psychology of Death* (2d. ed) (New York: Springer Publishing Co., Inc., 1992), 102.

[5] Nagy, *supra* note 2, at 97; Goodman, *supra* note 2, at 313.

[6] Rando, *supra* note 3, at 159.

[7] Burl E. Gilliland, and Richard K. James, *Crisis Intervention Strategies* (California: Brooks/Cole, 1993), 414.

[8] Rando, *supra* note 3, at 159.

[9] Del Zoppo, *supra* note 2, at 55-56; Rando, *supra* note 3, at 159-60; Alan D. Wolfelt "Helping Children Cope With Grief," *Thanatos* 16, no. 3 (1991): 17-18.

[10] Del Zoppo, *supra* note 2, at 53, 55; Nagy, *supra* note 2, at 96-97; Joyce Bluestone, "School-Based Peer Therapy to Facilitate Mourning in Latency-Age Children Following Sudden Parental Death" in *Play Therapy with Children in Crisis*, ed. N.B. Webb (New York: The Guilford Press, 1991), 254.

[11] Rando, *supra* note 3, at 160-61; Del Zoppo, *supra* note 2, 55; Bluestone, *supra* note 10, at 254.

[12] Nagy, *supra* note 2, at 98; Saraway, *supra* note 1, at 179-80; Rando, *supra* note 3, at 155.

[13] Bluestone, *supra* note 10, at 255.

[14] Bluestone, *supra* note 10, at 255; Nagy, *supra* note 2, at 98, Rando, *supra* note 3, at 155-56; Del Zoppo, *supra* note 2, at 11, 16-17.

[15] Gilliland and James, *supra* note 7, at 414; Rando, *supra* note 3, at 164-65; Del Zoppo, *supra* note 2, at 42, 56; Bluestone, *supra* note 10, at 254-55.

[16] J. William Worden, *Grief Counseling and Grief Therapy: A Handbook for the Mental Health Practitioner* (New York: Springer Publishing Co., Inc., 1982).

[17] Nagy, *supra* note 2, at 79.

[18] Gilliland and James, *supra* note 7, at 3.

[19] *Id.*

[20] Nancy Boyd Webb, (ed.), *Play Therapy with Children in Crisis* (New York: The Guilford Press, 1991), 27.

[21] *Id.* at 29.

[22] *Id.*

[23] Gilliland and James, *supra* note 7, at 429.

[24] *Id.*; Webb, *supra* note 20, at 33-34.

[25] Lori Stahl, "Music Therapy and the Grieving Child." *Thanatos*, 15, no. 3 (1990): 14.

[26] Webb, *supra* note 20, at 31-32; Gilliland and James, *supra* note 7, at 430; Stahl, *supra* note 24, at 14.

[27] Webb, *supra* note 20, at 34-35; Stahl, *supra* note 24, at 14.

[28] Gilliland and James, *supra* note 7, at 430.

[29] *Id.*

[30] Webb, *supra* note 20, at 37.

[31] *Id.* at 35-37.

[32] Nagy, *supra* note 2, at 98; Rando, *supra* note 3, at 170-72; Gilliland and James, *supra* note 7, at 429, Webb, *supra* note 20, at 27-28; Stahl, *supra* note 24, at 14.

CHAPTER 6

When Adolescents Grieve

I. Introduction

While much can be said concerning the care with which one must approach grief counseling with children, it must not be assumed that entrance into adolescence will somehow, magically, cause the emerging adult to accept the death of a loved one with philosophical complacency. The adolescent years, under the best of circumstances, are anything but philosophical or complacent. They are fraught with their own age-specific trials and tribulations.

II. Characteristics of Adolescence

The emerging teenager can be seen as entering a new life stage replete with its own identity, status, and experiences. As a neophyte in the teenage culture, the young person may find this experience both pleasant and/or stressful. New roles, responsibilities, and expectations can invariably result in stress and confusion. The ubiquitous allurement of sex, drugs, and alcohol can place the adolescent in a compromising position.[1] He or she must struggle with the alternatives presented. There can be refusal, compliance, or experimentation, with peer pressure often being a significant factor.

Adolescence is a time of physical, emotional, and psychological metamorphosis. Personality, sexuality, and an increased quest for independence are both emerging within, and converging upon, the unsuspecting youngster who is so happy not to be "a kid" any longer. It is a period in one's life characterized by mood, personality, and behavioral idiosyncrasies generously endowed with a rebellious spirit.[2] Adolescence is a part of the life cycle during which "[individuals] struggle to find self-identity, and this struggle is often accompanied by erratic behavior."[3] Anna Freud concluded that adolescence is inherently a time of disharmony and disrupted equilibrium.[4] This is to be considered normal for this period of the youngster's life.

Thus, it is apparent that the teenager, not unlike the middle-age parent discussed in Chapter 2, may very well have a preexisting collection of stressors when he or she learns of the death of a loved one.

75

Like the parent, teenagers may be engrossed in their own daily turmoil when, on top of all this, the death event arrives to further intrude upon their lives. And intrude it will, for most adolescents do not concern themselves with concepts of death.[5] They are more concerned with their immediate daily lives and near future. They tend to share the American cultural propensity to avoid the topic of death; it is too far removed from their present concerns.[6]

III. Adolescent Reaction to Death

With this synoptic background in place, the thrust of this chapter will be to explore the teenage grief experience and its characteristic behaviors in an effort to better understand the ramifications and pitfalls. This chapter will suggest appropriate and effective age-specific bereavement interventions.

The astute bereavement counselor must keep in mind, at all times, that despite occasional unpleasant behaviors teenagers are essentially tender and vulnerable and quite capable of feeling the deep hurt caused by death. However, when death can no longer be avoided, when the adolescent is confronted with a significant loss through death, how is it interpreted? One expert suggests that: "[f]or the adolescent, death just doesn't make sense. Most everything in our society emphasizes the power of life."[7] Death makes no sense because, as observed, most teenagers do not integrate this concept into their daily thinking patterns. Since cultural norms tend to treat talk of death as a social taboo, only life-related topics remain prominent in one's mind.[8] The result is that the adolescent experiences a sense of confusion.

The teenager's current life is undergoing significant changes. The change caused by the death of a loved one is not only unexpected, in most cases, but is powerful in its permanence and irreversibility. The adolescent can experience most changes with an air of hope that things will get better. With the finality of death, hope is stifled, and even the near future is to some extent forever changed.

The adolescent's reaction to crisis is a product of the youngster's "expectations, goals, and belief systems," and the extent of one's vulnerability.[9] This definition is critical in that the conceptualization and integration of death is far removed from the adolescent's thoughts and beliefs, thus leaving him or her quite vulnerable to a flood of new and confusing, even frightening, feelings. Because adolescents are, to an extent, insulated from conceptualizing death at this point in their lives, they lack a basic understanding of it and its nature and implications. They will, however, experience the same grief reactions as adults do (see Chapter 1), and they will experience pain and distress. They will sense that their safety and security are being threatened and they will feel an uncomfortable sense of helplessness. All of this contributes to the general confusion that they find themselves cloaked in.[10]

Initially, adolescents will react to death with disbelief: "It isn't real." "How could that be?" "I can't even picture it." Disbelief is a first-line coping mechanism used to deal with the finality of an irreversible loss.[11]

Coupled with disbelief, and commonly occurring when the death event is sudden or unexpected, is denial. Denial is a negation that the death event actually happened, and it helps to cushion the teenager from the reality of the loss as well as from loss of control and thoughts of one's own mortality. It is an ego mechanism used to avoid a reality that is painful. Specifically, denial protects the young griever from (1) the facts about the loss; (2) its finality and irreversibility; and (3) confronting exactly what that death means to them at that particular time. It is important for the bereavement counselor to note that, in most cases involving teenagers and death events, the observable denial usually is manifested in some form of limited distortion and usually is not a matter of total delusion. The adolescent may opt to continue this denial through periodic "selective forgetting" or, more seriously, by blocking visual images. The extreme takes place when adolescents totally deny that the death occurred at all or that the relationship with the lost loved one never existed. It would be helpful for the bereavement counselor to bear in mind that belief and disbelief fluctuate.

Consequently, it is important and beneficial for adolescents to have their feelings validated and be given the opportunity to reality test their feelings. In a real sense, do the events surrounding the loss really justify feelings held?[12]

Frequently, a current initial reaction to loss is a sense of shock that, as described in Chapter 2, is nature's own form of emotional anesthesia. It can control the balance of how much reality one can absorb at any given time. It serves as a buffer and can shut out some

77

aspects of reality. Recollections of sequences or events may be obscure or unavailable. Some may find shock as a "gift" that helped them get through something that would have been too difficult to comprehend at the moment. As the realization of the event begins to emerge, shock subsides, permitting denial to surface and continue to protect the mourner until he or she can gradually absorb the full realization of the death loss.[13]

At this point, adolescents will experience many of the same grief responses that adults will exhibit. They can begin to perceive future events touched by the loss of the loved one, for example, a young lady can picture not having her father to escort her on her wedding day. However, these adult responses, to an extent, will be compromised by the variety of pre-existing adolescent issues and concerns previously mentioned. The teenager is usually uncomfortable with mourning and emotional expression. While the youngster may feel a need for inclusion in post-death activities such as dialogues, funerary and memorialization planning, and appropriate mourning processes, there will be times when her or she will prefer privacy. This need should be understood and respected. The adolescent has to sort out his or her own understanding of the loss, the events of the death, his or her own role as a mourner, and what is expected of him or her.[14]

While adolescents normally exhibit a broad range of behaviors, the death event usually forces anger to surface. In essence, it is anger at the death itself ("He was so young," "How could this happen?"), a searching for meaning, an effort to "make sense" of the death. There may be anger at not having had "control," i.e., not having the ability to have prevented the death, or even at the deceased for having left.[15]

Along with anger, teenagers may exhibit strong feelings of guilt after the loss of a loved one. These feelings may be a way of masking feelings of helplessness or may even be used to punish oneself for real or perceived past transgressions. Guilt also may play a role in the adolescent remembering certain events lest they be forgotten and the deceased dishonored.[16]

Adolescents often exhibit guilt because they may feel that they might have been able to alter the course of events, that maybe they were somehow responsible for the death. Again, the issue of control can play a significant role in this kind of grief-guilt. The fact that they survived and the deceased didn't (for example, automobile accident or fire) can lead to feelings of "survivor guilt." This is particularly prevalent among survivors of traumatic circumstances (for example, suicide, homicide, or war) who may be suffering from Posttraumatic Stress Disorder (PTSD).[17]

Another aspect of guilt to be considered occurs when there have been strong negative feelings within a close relationship. In most close relationships, positive and negative feelings can coexist; there usually is a given amount of ambivalence. With the post-death idealization of the lost loved one, this ambivalence can lead to strong guilt for having had these negative feelings.[18]

While several factors can elicit feelings of post-death guilt, many of these feelings are circumstantial and irrational.[19] The bereavement counselor can assist the survivors to reality test their feelings for validity. If guilt still remains, the wise counselor should make a referral to a professional therapist for treatment. The roles of anger and guilt will be developed further in Chapters 11, 12, and 13.

IV. Danger Signs

As previously mentioned, adolescents normally may display fluctuating or rebellious behavior. However, during a period of bereavement, certain behaviors may emerge that can be considered dangerous and will require careful observation. Underlying feelings such as low self-esteem, sadness, guilt, helplessness, perceived rejection, and an intense denial of the reality of the death can cause the adolescent to exhibit aggressiveness and antisocial behavior as well as risk-taking and even suicidal ideation.[20]

In situations of "high-risk denial," one expert observes, "we see the teen griever exhibiting a determined effort to avoid the reality of the death at any and all costs even with induced harm to himself or herself."[21] This behavior must be taken seriously when there are repeated occurrences without a reduction of "intensity, frequency, and duration, as time moves further away from the death occurrence."[22] If the survivor's denial is seen to increase as time goes on, then prompt, professional intervention will be needed and an appropriate referral must be made.[23]

Some of the danger signs that can indicate a suicidal ideation are:
- displays of strong anger or rage toward the deceased, intense feelings of guilt and denial, frequent visits to the cemetery;

79

- use of alcohol or drugs;

- change in peer and social interactions;

- giving away significant personal possessions, feelings of sadness, depression, lack of hope, lack of self-esteem;

- displays of extreme risk-taking behaviors within months of the death event; and

- verbalization of suicidal thoughts.[24]

These danger signs must not be ignored, and students who exhibit them should be treated by a professional therapist or certified crisis intervention counselor.

V. Interventions

In developing bereavement counseling strategies, school officials should bear in mind that while adolescents will have many of the same responses to death as adults, these responses may be affected by various typical, age-specific problems. The bereavement program outlined in Chapter 1 is an effective and comprehensive format for adults and students who have acquired the adult cognitive and conceptual orientation toward death. For students who have not yet reached that level, an alternative format is suggested below. This format also can be used when time and resource constraints do not permit a 10-session program.

The major portion of the program in Chapter 1 should be retained personnel, resources, facilities, parental notification and permission, contracting, and goals. The point of departure occurs at the 10-Session Model. Here a six-session model is presented in its place. The bereavement team can assess the grieving population as well as available resources to decide which model is appropriate for any given group. Groups can be led by one or two trained facilitators who are committed to attending each of the six sessions.

Six-Session Model[25]

Session 1. Getting Acquainted

This initial session should be used to provide group members with the opportunity to become acquainted with each other and with the group leader (facilitator). Students should introduce themselves and share with the group some of their experiences concerning their loss.

Students may be asked if this death event has been the most difficult experience in their lives. They should be encouraged to name the most difficult aspect of the loss.

Students should be given the opportunity to ask questions about the group or about the experience of loss in a general sense.

Each student should consider a personal goal he or she would like to accomplish as a member of the group.

Students should be asked to share their memories concerning their response upon hearing of the death of their loved one.

Students should be given time for continued discussion. The session can end with each student reflecting on previous losses that they've encountered and have recovered from. The suggestion can be made that students consider their past losses and their recovery from them in view of their response to this present loss of a loved one.

Students should be reminded of their agreement (contract) for confidentiality and should be praised for having completed Session One.

Session 2. Comprehending the Loss

This session can be used to explore how the adolescent mourner perceives the loss of a loved one in his or her life. With facilitator assistance, the students will have the opportunity to enhance their reality and comprehension of the loss through death.

Students can use storytelling as a vehicle to exchange views and concepts concerning their perspective of loss at this juncture in their lives. Using dialogue and interaction, students can convey aspects of the relationship while exploring facts of the death event.

The facilitator may initiate a general discussion concerning loss in an effort to have students open a dialogue concerning death-related issues.

Students should be encouraged to participate by stressing the idea that talking about death-related issues is not morbid when there is a purpose to it.

Students can be shown a video of a teen mourner or given a group exercise in which they can write topics such as their own concerns about death, compile a personal death history in which they can write down their experiences, or write an assessment of their own fear of death.

The session can close with the facilitator complimenting the members for their sincerity and expression of thoughts and feelings shared with the group.

Session 3. Exploring Post-Loss Feelings

The purpose of this session is to have teenagers gain an understanding that it is natural and appropriate to have reactions and strong personal feelings following a loss. By identifying one's feelings, the student is able to "own" the feeling and can better personalize his or her loss. Repeating, this procedure will help the student to better acknowledge the loss and can pave the way for its eventual acceptance.

This session would be a good opportunity to reflect on previous sessions, tie-up loose ends, and answer leftover questions. It also could be used to evaluate the first two sessions and determine if any changes should be made.

The session can open with the distribution of a facilitator-generated handout designed to have students identify their own personal reactions to the loss in question. This could cover physical, thought, behavioral, emotional, and relational reactions.

Students can share these reactions and feelings with the group. It may be useful to review the normal expressions of grief (see Chapter 1) in order to reassure students just how normal their feelings are. It is interesting to note that many "family patterns" of dealing with loss may emerge.

The session can be concluded by having students discuss what particular pattern of dealing with loss that they view personally for themselves. Students should be encouraged to evaluate how they are able to express post-loss feelings and reactions. Students may wish to compare differences and similarities with the other group members with respect to their comprehension and expression of the loss of a loved one.

Students should be given an awareness of how valuable it is to get in touch with their feelings, as well as the value of having someone to listen to them. During the time between sessions, students should try to identify those people who are most helpful in listening to their feelings.

Session 4. The Adjustment to Change Caused by Loss

The focus of this session is to have students identify the various changes that the present loss has brought into their lives. Students will be asked to identify primary and secondary losses caused by the death loss. For example,

Primary loss: My best friend died.

Secondary loss: The one who always defended me is gone.

The facilitator will discuss patterns of recovery with the students to help them make the necessary adjustment(s). For example,

Status of loss: I lost my best friend and defender.

Status of change: My support system (defense) is gone.

Possible alternative: Maybe I will find someone else who will like me and be on my side.

Awareness: I am most comfortable when I can share my feelings with someone special whom I can trust to support me.

Students should follow this with a group discussion about change. The facilitator should introduce such topics as: What kind of change can be accepted easily? What kind of change can a death loss effect in your life? Which kinds of losses are easier to recover from? and What kind of support is available to you when you are confronted with changes through loss? Students should include in their discussion a self-perception of themselves when confronted with a loss change. What would they be like on a day that they would be struggling with change? How do friends and family perceive their capacity to handle change? What do they feel is the simplest means of adapting to change? What is their perception of a satisfactory recovery from change caused by loss?

Students can incorporate these questions into a written exercise and try to assess the extent of recovery they are experiencing as a result of the loss caused by this death event.

The facilitator should conclude the session with an observation about the types of losses and changes the students have sustained in their lives, as well as a complimentary remark about the recoveries that have been made.

Session 5. Post-Loss Coping Patterns

The purpose of this session is to assist the students in their search for recovery and return to happy living. By helping adolescents to explore their coping patterns, as well as to develop an awareness of personal pitfalls, these youngsters can develop an appreciation for the progress that they are making with respect to the death-related loss. These young adults need an inventory of skills to help them successfully cope with the changes that are necessary during a difficult time in their lives.

Students will explore the concept of coping patterns as being "diversions to reduce stress." Some patterns are beneficial, others can be negative or neutral, and still others can be harmful. Students should explore the five basic ways people use to cope with stress.

1. People tend to comfort themselves in a physical sense by drinking or eating, or in some kind of physical activity.

2. Sometimes people will comfort themselves in private, using isolation and withdrawal.

3. People often may call out to another person to seek companionship or to form a new relationship.

4. Some people are able to approach the situation directly and ask for advice and seek further education.

5. Sometimes people will engage in certain risk-taking behaviors, such as increased drinking, drug use, or reckless actions. As previously mentioned, risk-taking behaviors are a special concern with teenage grievers.

The facilitator should have students generate a personal inventory worksheet on which they can list and evaluate the various coping styles that they have used in their lives. Have the students categorize their coping behaviors in terms of the five classifications listed above.

The facilitator should have students explain why their behaviors may fall into their respective categories. Students should discuss what may have influenced their choice of behavior, positively or negatively, as well as identify healthy and unhealthy patterns. Students should discuss some of the possible outcomes of problematic coping behaviors.

The session should conclude with a discussion of the individual coping behaviors that were exhibited at the time of the present death event, and how these behaviors affected the students. Emphasis should be given to the more positive aspects of these behaviors.

Session 6. Assessment of Learning and Recovery

The purpose of this session is to help the members of the group review their lives up to this point in time and to have them verbalize their aspirations and thoughts for the future. Almost all adolescents have an innate desire for recovery and returning to normal living. The wise facilitator will be attuned to the various hints that may be given when someone needs additional help to move on. Sometimes, the adolescent needs "permission" to return back to normal living. This can be provided by the help and counseling alliance of a good facilitator.

The students should be made aware that the final task on the road to recovery is to learn to let go of the former attachment. The survivor must be able to establish a new relationship with the deceased. The griever must review the events of the loss and determine what has changed and what has not.

This session will complete the self-exploration of such questions as: What occurred internally? What was your reaction? What were you feeling? What changes took place? What were your coping patterns?

Students should be given a written assignment to assess what they have learned about themselves resulting from this counseling experience. They also should try to assess the extent of their recovery.

The facilitator should initiate a final discussion in which participants can express what they were initially looking for from the group. Did they have any fears about joining the group? How did this loss affect their self-esteem? Which members of the group were supports for them? Would they recommend this kind of group to others?

All participants in the group must realize that the final session of the group is itself a loss and must be addressed. Students may be invited to offer a final message to the entire group.

The facilitator should thank the group and praise them for the courage they've shown and for the work they've accomplished.

VI. Summary

A. Characteristics of Adolescence

    1. New status and identity

    2. New roles and expectations

    3. Physical, emotional, and psychological changes

    4. Erratic behavior, rebelliousness

B. Adolescent Grief

    1. Death not in immediate thoughts

    2. Death doesn't make sense

    3. Vulnerable to pain, deep hurt, and new and confusing feelings

    4. Safety and security threatened, sense of helplessness

C. Adolescent Reaction to Death Event

    1. Disbelief

    2. Denial

    3. Shock

    4. Realization of death loss

    5. Awareness of a changed future due to loss

    6. Anger

    7. Ambivalence

    8. Guilt/Survivor guilt

    9. Sense of loss of control

D. Needs of Grieving Adolescent

    1. Inclusion in dialogues, funerary and memorialization planning

    2. Privacy

    3. Need to sort out own understanding of the loss

    4. Search for meaning

    5. Understanding of what is expected of him or her

E. Danger Signs

    1. Aggression, antisocial behavior

    2. Low self-esteem, depression, sadness

    3. Giving away valued personal possessions

    4. Change in peer and social interactions

    5. Extreme risk-taking behaviors

    6. Talking about suicide

F. Suggested Interventions Six-Session Model

    1. Getting Acquainted

        a. Introductions

        b. Death-related questions

        c. Establish a personal goal

        d. Establish a group contract

    2. Comprehending the Loss

        a. Adolescents' perception of loss

        b. Enhance reality

        c. Group discussion, dialogue, and interaction

    3. Exploring Post-Loss Feelings

        a. Natural and appropriate to have feelings

b. Identify one's own personal reaction

c. Possible emergence of "family pattern" of reacting to grief

4. Adjustment to Change Caused by Loss

    a. Identify changes caused by loss

    b. Identify secondary losses

    c. Recovery patterns

    d. Developing an awareness of need(s)

    e. Assess recovery

5. Post-Loss Coping Patterns

    a. Behaviors

    Searching for recovery and return to normal living

    Comfort self physically (food, drink)

    Withdrawal/isolation

    Call out to others

    Direct approach — ask for advice, education

    Risk-taking behavior(s)

    b. Strategies

    Develop personal inventory of coping styles

    Discuss why behaviors fall into certain categories

    Discuss what influenced behavior(s)

    Identify healthy behavior(s)

    Discuss outcomes of problematic behaviors

6. Assessment of Learning and Recovery

    a. Life review

    b. Aspirations and thoughts for the future

c. Letting go of former attachments

d. Determine what has changed and what hasn't

e. Assess what one has learned

f. Evaluate recovery

g. Offer final message to the group

89

Endnotes

[1] Carel B. Germain, *Human Behavior in the Social Environment* (New York: Columbia University Press, 1991), 352-53.

[2] *Id.* at 354.

[3] Robert L. Barker, *The Social Work Dictionary 2d ed.* (Washington, D.C.: The NASW Press, 1991), 5.

[4] Judith Marks Mishne, *Clinical Work with Adolescents* (New York: The Free Press, 1986).

[5] Robert Kastenbaum, "Time and Death in Adolescence" in *The Meaning of Death* ed. H. Feifel (New York: McGraw Hill, 1959), 99-113.; Robert, Kastenbaum, *The Psychology of Death* 2d ed. (New York: Springer Publishing Co., Inc., 1992).

[6] Kastenbaum, "Time and Death," *supra* note 5, at 104, 111-12; Kastenbaum, *The Psychology of Death, supra* note 5, at 120, 127.

[7] Patrick M. Del Zoppo, *PASSAGES: A Guidebook for TEENS in GRIEF — their Parents, Friends, and Caregivers* (Patrick Del Zoppo Associates, New York: The Richmond Institute, 1993), 12.

[8] Kastenbaum, "Time and Death," *supra* note 5, at 111-12; J. William, Worden *Grief Counseling and Grief Therapy: A Handbook for the Mental Health Practitioner* (New York: Springer Publishing Co., Inc., 1982), 13.

[9] Brian J. McConville, "Assessment, Crisis Intervention, and Time Limited Cognitive Therapy with Children and Adolescents Grieving the Loss of a Loved One," in *Crisis Intervention Handbook Assessment, Treatment, and Research*, ed. A. Roberts (California: Wadsworth, Inc., 1990), 31.

[10] Burl E. Gilliland, and Richard K. James, *Crisis Intervention Strategies* (California: Brooks/Cole, 1993), 415; Del Zoppo, *supra* note 7, at 12-13.

[11] Del Zoppo, *supra* note 7, at 14.

[12] *Id.* at 43-44; Mishne *supra* note 4, at 348; Therese A. Rando, *Grief, Dying, and Death: Clinical Interventions for Caregivers* (Illinois: Research Press Co., 1984), 162.

[13] Rando, *supra* note 12, at 29.

[14] *Id.* at 162; Gilliland and James, *supra* note 10, at 415.

[15] Rando, *supra* note 12, at 31; Del Zoppo, *supra* note 7, at 17, 23.

[16] Therese A. Rando, *Treatment of Complicated Mourning* (Illinois: Research Press Co., 1993), 478.

[17] *Id.* at 481; Gilliland and James, *supra* note 10, at 179; Laura Mufson, Donna Moreau, Myrna Weissman, Gerald L. Klerman*, Interpersonal Psychotherapy for Depressed Adolescents* (New York: The Guilford Press, 1993), 91.

[18] Worden, *supra* note 8, at 30; Rando, *supra* note 16, at 480-81.

[19] Worden, *supra* note 8, at 42.

[20] Frank J. Bruno, *Psychological Symptoms* (New York: John Wiley and Sons, Inc., 1993), 196; McConville, *supra* note 9, at 38; Del Zoppo, *supra* note 7, at 65; Germain, *supra* note 1, at 366-67.

[21] Del Zoppo, *supra* note 7, at 65.

[22] *Id.*

[23] *Id.*

[24] *Id.* at 64-65; Germain, *supra* note 1, at 360; Bruno, *supra* note 20, at 196.

[25] This model has been adapted with permission from *PASSAGES: A Guidebook for TEENS in GRIEF — their Parents, Friends, and Caregivers* by Patrick M. Del Zoppo, pages 104-42, ©1993 by Patrick Del Zoppo Associates (New York: The Richmond Institute). All rights reserved.

CHAPTER 7

Depression

I. Introduction

Depression is a term that is widely used in contemporary society today. One often hears a friend or associate say, "I'm so depressed today" or "it was so depressing." What do they mean by that? Are they using the expression correctly? Some form of clarification would seem appropriate. In this chapter, the writer will seek to provide an inclusive clinical narrative while, at the same time, offering a functional, everyday understanding of the term.

According to Lilly (2001, p. 15)[1] approximately one out of every 8 or 12.5 percent of the American population will experience some form of depression in the course of their lifetime. While not as frequent as the common cold, depression is not an uncommon condition. There are, however, variations. The depression we encounter in everyday life, i.e., feeling sad over a bad day; the feelings of being "down in the dumps" or experiencing the "blues"; or the emptiness we feel after suffering the loss of a family member or friend, are *real* emotions and can be disturbing. However, they are "natural" feelings and can be experienced by every healthy human being. These feelings tend to run their course and pass without the necessity of medical or pharmacological intervention (Pfizer 2000, p.3).[2]

The depression that is of a more disturbing nature, which truly mediates the daily life of the sufferer, is one that necessitates close attention. It is this serious, or clinical, depression that can last for extended periods of time. It can affect one's thinking, bodily functions, and behavior (Greist 1996, pp. 4-5).[3]

II. What Is Depression?

When one considers depression, in a clinical sense, one must consider a serious depressive, medical condition that can vary in both severity as well as length of duration. Depression affects specific mood and thought patterns as well as behavior and even bodily functions. It must be taken seriously because it can alter one's ability to function on a daily basis. In the extreme, depression can even be life-

93

threatening when it results in a suicidal ideation. (Pfizer 2000, p. 2) (Greist 1996, pp. 4-5).[4] Fortunately, most forms of depression can be successfully treated. However, the condition may be subject to later, recurring episodes (Lilly 2001, p. 15).[5] Suffice to say that depression is serious, is manageable and *should* be treated.

In order to be most effective, the reader is well-advised to become familiar with the classic symptoms of depression as well as to pursue competent treatment as early as possible.

III. Symptoms of Depression

- depressed mood	- low self-esteem
- lack of interest or pleasure	- decline in work functions
- irritability	- sense of helplessness
- behavioral changes	- sadness
- loss of weight	- sense of hopelessness
- change in eating habits	- change in sleep
- restlessness	- feelings of guilt
- lack of energy	-death-related thoughts
- difficulty concentrating	- suicidal thoughts

(*Diagnostic and Statistical Manual of Mental Disorders*, 4th ed. 1994, p. 327).[6]

IV. Kinds of Depression

Although it is abundantly clear that the purpose of this text is for use in general counseling rather than as a guide for chronic and profound clinical treatment, it would, nevertheless, do no harm to consider a few of the technical aspects of depression.

First of all, depression is officially classified as a mood disorder, i.e., it is characterized as a condition whose predominant feature is a disturbance in mood (*Diagnostic and Statistical Manual of Mental Disorders*, 4th ed., 1994, p. 317).[7] Depression is divided into several distinct classifications, each having specific as well as similar characteristics. In this treatment, the writer intends only to "scratch the surface" in order to give the reader a realistic picture as to just what both the griever and the counselor have to work on, together, to resolve. This will be done, of course, in a general sense. For the purposes of this text, the reader will consider *Major Depressive Disorder, Dysthymic Disorder,* and *Adjustment Disorder with Depressed Mood.*

Major Depressive Disorder: This condition is indicated by at least one Major Depressive Episode of a minimum of two weeks in duration. It is characterized by either depressed mood or loss of pleasure/ interest and at least four of the Symptoms of Depression listed in section III. The diagnosis of Major Depressive Disorder is usually not entertained until the symptoms persist beyond a post-loss period of at least two months. With this disorder, the depressed mood occurs almost daily and is present for almost the entire day (*Diagnostic and Statistical Manual of Mental Disorders*, 4th ed., 1994, pp. 317, 327, 343, 684).[8]

Dysthymic Disorder: Similar to the Major Depressive Disorder, the Dysthymic Disorder is often diagnosed when the depressive characteristics are chronic, persist for many years, and are less severe in nature. (*Diagnostic and Statistical Manual of Mental Disorders*, 4th ed., 1994, pp. 345, 346, 349).[9]

Adjustment Disorder with Depressed Mood: Essentially, adjustment disorders are identified as a result of the development of significant behavioral or emotional symptoms that develop within three months following the onset of a recognizable psychosocial stressor(s). A salient characteristic would be either a marked "impairment in social or occupational (academic) functioning" or an excessive distress that goes beyond what would ordinarily be expected as a result of exposure to the particular stressor(s). It can be specified as acute if the duration does not exceed six months or chronic if it endures six months or longer. It may be further coded *with Depressed Mood* when there is a pronounced depressed mood, a sense of sadness/tearfulness and hopelessness (*Diagnostic and Statistical Manual of Mental Disorders*, 4th ed., 1994, pp. 623, 626) (Keller et al. 1994, p.19).[10]

V. What Causes Depression?

Inasmuch as depression can manifest itself in various forms and severities, it appears safe to say that its cause(s) also might be diverse. Occasionally, depression can be easily attributed to a specific reason or event. Other times, it may appear without apparent cause. The relative, contemporary literature holds a few contributory causes (Greist 1996, pp. 6-7).[11] For the reader's basic background, four of these theories will be briefly outlined here.

Biological Theory: Current literature indicates that there may be certain physiological causes of depression. Biochemical imbalance is thought to be a major factor in the disorder. The human brain contains upward of billions of nerves, neurons, that intercommunicate via electrochemical impulses, i.e., chemicals called neurotransmitters are present in the areas between neurons and are employed to convey various information from one to another. Some of these neurotransmitters are thought to affect mood. Consequently, altering their levels is believed to positively affect one's mood. Genetics, personality, life events, and environmental substances also are seen as possible variables and/or precipitants of neurotransmitter levels (Keller et al. 1994, p. 22) (Greist 1996, p. 7).[12]

Psychoanalytic Theory: The brainchild of Sigmund Freud, psychoanalytic theory is predicated upon the belief that humans pass through various developmental stages in their journey through life. Unresolved unpleasant, traumatic, or disappointing childhood experiences can possibly lead to one's developing depression and, thus, make the condition traceable back to early childhood. Early feelings of pain, low self-esteem, hopelessness, helplessness, etc., can fuel a future depressive condition. Subsequent, indicative losses or failures may recall childhood feelings of "powerlessness" (Keller et al., 1994, p. 22).[13]

Cognitive Theory: Relating to thought, cognitive theory credits the depressive state as a result of erroneous or distorted thoughts of one's self-image. These negative fabrications can produce the telltale feelings of hopelessness and helplessness that are earmarks of the depressive mood. There appears to be no let up on the negativity for the future either. There is also the chance that various self-defeating behaviors can result from such thinking and cause further depression. Cognitive therapy is a structured, solution-based treatment that has been found to be effective in depression treatment (Keller et al., 1994, p. 23) (Greist 1996, p. 9).[14]

Interpersonal Theory: The interpersonal approach is different from the preceding three theories. While the initial theories are predicated, essentially, upon the individual and his/her thoughts and repertoire of experiences, the interpersonal approach is predicated upon the individual's depression as a factor in a "between people setting." There is almost a "chicken-or-egg" aspect also. On the one hand, it can be seen how interpersonal complexities can result in depression, it is also true, on the other hand, that a person's depression can lead him/her to problems in one's interpersonal relationships as well. The aim of treatment in this instance is to reduce symptoms, build self-esteem, and focus upon effective management of interpersonal and social relationships (Keller et al. 1994, p. 23) (Greist 1996, p. 9).[15]

It should, by now, be apparent that depression has many aspects and no one, single, cause. Each theory can explain only part of the problem. A universal, all conclusive, theory still eludes us.

VI. Grief vs. Depression

When confronted with the loss of a loved one, it is not uncommon for survivors to experience many of the same symptoms associated with "classic" depression (review *Reactions in the Normal Grief Experience* in Chapter 1). This is quite normal and should not cause alarm. However, it is not usually of sufficient severity to merit a diagnosis of any of the more serious mood disorders.

While the reader is directed to *Key Differences Between Grief and Depression*, found in Appendix D, it is worth the effort to excerpt and consider some of the salient areas of confusion.

In the area of mood states, it becomes obvious that serious depression is present when there is a consistently negative side of everyday functioning such as communication, general interest in things, sexual interest, verbal output, etc. Anger may be found to be internally directed without openness or hostility. Also, depression is indicated when the survivor experiences severe insomnia and is subject to early morning awakenings.

One of the most indicative characteristics of the presence of serious depression is found in the survivor's own self-concept. He/she may be preoccupied with self and sees self as intrinsically worthless and/or bad. Serious depression is always indicated when a survivor develops a detectable suicidal ideation, i.e., a desire to commit suicide, distinct planning, an absence of support, and a refusal to contract with others. (The reader is encouraged to review Chapter 8, "Suicide," sections II, III and IV.)

Serious depression is further indicated when the survivor fails to respond to most normal stimuli and may appear to be generally anhedonic, or lacking in experiencing pleasure. The depressed person is usually "self-contained" and rarely reaches out to others.

What is important for the reader to remember is that while the grief experience does entail some amount of depression, it does not usually entail the more serious clinical depression (Del Zoppo 1993, p. 65).[16]

VII. Dangers of Depression

At this point in the discussion on depression, it should be abundantly clear to the reader that depression is a mood disorder fraught with emotional pain, sadness, frustration and even certain dangers.

The first threat or danger that depression poses is, of course, to one's sense of happiness and well-being. The air of "mental freedom" is taken away and replaced with a sort of "cloak of shadow." In other words, the individual is no longer carefree and happy.

Furthermore, when the reader reviews sections II and III, of this chapter, it becomes quite clear that depression can threaten the individual's everyday life. One can become restless, irritable, sleepless, pleasureless, and/or morbid. The extent of the dysfunction is determined by the severity of the depression. Consequently, one's employment, productivity, mood, interpersonal relationships, and even health are jeopardized.

The greatest danger attributed to depression is the loss of life by suicide. As indicated in Chapter 8, the key element common to all attempts at self-destruction is depression—an element that can be masked by other symptoms or problems (Fishman 1988, pp. 159-60).[17] In the suicidal ideation, the depression suffered by the victim causes him/her to decompensate or "sink" to a point where the helplessness and hopelessness is of such magnitude that suicide appears to make sense to the victim (Fishman 1988, pp. 159-60).[18] Hence the necessity of recognizing the telltale signs of depression, and the necessity to act upon it. If an individual appears to be sufficiently depressed to perhaps be suicidal, one must make this known to someone trained to deal with it immediately. One must remember that when there is apparent danger, with respect to life, confidentiality usually can be put aside and the counselor is held harmless (Gilliland and James 1993, p. 136).[19] The author suggests that the counselor check local laws and ordinances.

Consequently, it should be abundantly clear to the reader that depression is a mood disorder that mixes suffering with potential dangers.

VIII. Treatment of Depression

Inasmuch as the reader has seen that depression may have a variety of causes, it stands to reason that there also may be multiple treatment modalities available as well. A few of these treatment modalities will be briefly described in this chapter. It is important to note that the therapies described here must be undertaken by qualified mental health practitioners only!

Psychotherapy: Psychotherapy is the oral or "talking" intervention often used to resolve or reduce dysfunctional behavior. A treatment, in which, usually, no prescription medication is used, this modality does require one to be honest in his/her sharing of thoughts and feelings with the counselor (Keller et al. 1994, p. 40).[20] Psychotherapy "types" may be identified by their various goal-based orientations.

a. Supportive Therapy: Probably the most common form of counseling used, this modality is based on a one-on-one support model that reassures, sets limits, advises, and establishes parameters for patient behavior. It is also useful in the development of various patient social skills (Keller et al. 1994, pp. 40-1).[21]

b. Behavioral Therapy: This modality, predicated upon the theory that the absence of positive reinforcement is a root cause of depression, seeks to maximize the positive aspects of the patient's life while minimizing other aspects such a trauma and separation. The intention is

99

to have the patient learn to alter his/her behavior and, thus, own one's life (Keller et al. 1994, p. 41).[22]

c. *Cognitive Therapy*: Basically a thought-altering process, this modality seeks to alleviate the patient's aberrant thoughts and behaviors that contribute to the depressive state. The patient is helped to negate negative thoughts while developing constructive and more positive self-perceptions. This format is more effective with moderate depression (Keller et al. 1994, p. 41).[23]

d. *Interpersonal Therapy*: The focal point(s) of this therapeutic modality are the interpersonal problems experienced by the depressed individual. The actual effect of the problem on the depression, itself, is not the primary interest here. The effective implementation of constructive interaction with others is the primary goal. Jointly, the individual and the therapist will identify current problematic interpersonal areas and develop strategies for improvement. Perhaps acceptable and appropriate interpersonal skills must be mastered. Behavior-modification techniques and communication skills are often explored (Keller et al. 1994, pp. 41-2).[24]

Each of these therapies may be conducted by a psychiatrist, psychologist, social worker, or licensed mental health counselor. In cases in which a psychiatrist or other physician is involved, anti-depressant medication may be used, if deemed necessary, as an adjunct to verbal therapy.

Chemotherapy (Pharmacological Intervention): Whenever any form of medication is used, medical supervision is a necessity. The use of antidepressants must always be under the direction of a physician, preferably a psychiatrist. In such cases, usually the first choice for treatment are the Selective Serotonin-Reuptake Inhibitors (SSRIs). These antidepressants apparently work primarily on the neurotransmitter serotonin, which carries messages throughout the nervous system as well as the brain, and appear to exhibit fewer side effects than the more complicated MAO Inhibitors and Tricyclic medications. The common denominator is that each of these drugs appear to raise the effectiveness level of serotonin in the brain that, in turn, appears to improve depression (Keller et al. 1994, pp. 35-6).[25]

Examples of SSRIs are ZOLOFT (Sertraline), PROZAC (Fluoxetine), and PAXIL (Paroxetine). EFFEXOR (Ventafaxine), a similar drug, affects both serotonin and norepinephrine transmitters in the brain. One drawback with EFFEXOR is that it can precipitate sustained high blood pressure and its use may require regular monitoring (Keller et al. 1994, pp. 36-7).[26]

In cases of severe depression, doctors have often recommended the use of Electroconvulsive Therapy (ECT). ECT, or "shock treatment," is believed to affect chemical changes in the brain, similar to those caused by antidepressant medications, which effectively treat depression safely and with minimal side effects. When depression poses very serious personal danger, then hospitalization is the treatment of choice and necessity (Keller et al. 1994, p. 39).[27]

Once again, effective treatment for depression may encompass one or all of these cited measures, individually or in concert with each other.

Depression in the Classroom/Workplace Model

Following is a flowchart model indicating the various stages and steps from intitial grief, reactions to, intervention and recovery. As one can see, there are four entry points into the system.

On the left side, we can see that a grief reaction can be precipitated by either a pre-death, anticipatory grief, or by an actual post-death grief. This grief can result in a measure of depression. Should this depression decompensate to a clinical suicidal ideation, then the individual must first go through *Crisis Intervention* for stabilization, i.e., the individual must be returned to the level of functioning that he/she exhibited before the death event, whatever that may have been.

Once stabilized, the individual can then proceed to grief counseling and/or depression therapy, as needed.

The reader also should note that the depressed individual who does not exhibit a suicidal ideation can continue along to grief counseling and/or depression therapy. Both routes should, ultimately, lead to *Recovery.*

It also is worthy to note that one can enter the system directly for *Grief Counseling* without *Depression*, as well as enter the system for *Depression* without *Grief Involvement.*

In any event, individuals entering at any one of the entry points should, ultimately, reach *Recovery.*

101

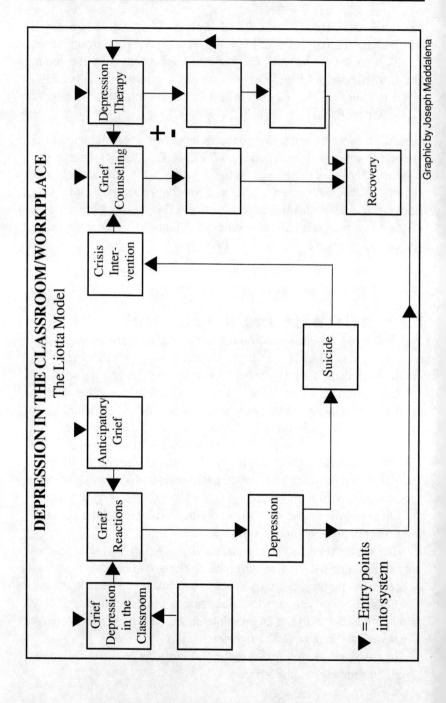

DEPRESSION IN THE CLASSROOM/WORKPLACE
The Liotta Model

Graphic by Joseph Maddalena

▶ = Entry points into system

IX. Summary

A. Depression

1. Widely "over-used" term

2. Natural disturbing feelings

3. Approximately 12.5 percent of Americans experience depression

B. What Is Depression?

1. A serious depressive, medical condition, a mood disorder

2. Can vary in length and severity

3. Affects mood, thought, behavior, and bodily functions

4. Can be life-threatening [Suicidal Ideation]

5. Although serious, depression is treatable and manageable

C. Symptoms of Depression

- depressed mood
- lack of interest or pleasure
- irritability
- behavioral changes
- weight loss
- change in eating habits
- restlessness
- lack of energy
- difficulty concentrating

- low self-esteem
- decline in work functions
- sense of helplessness
- sadness
- sense of hopelessness
- change in sleep
- feelings of guilt
- death-related thoughts
- suicidal thoughts

D. Kinds of Depression

1. Major Depressive Disorder

2. Dysthymic Disorder

3. Adjustment Disorder with Depressed Mood

4. Variations and combinations of above

E. Causes of Depression

1. Biological Theory

a. Neurotransmitters: serotonin, norepinephrine

b. Biochemical imbalance

c. Personality

d. Genetics

e. Environmental factors

2. Psychoanalytic Theory (Freudian)

a. Depression traceable back to childhood

b. Unresolved experiences can fuel future depression

c. Indicative losses' failures may recall "powerlessness"

3. Cognitive Theory

a. Relating to thought

b. Erroneous or distorted thoughts of one's self-image

c. Self-defeating behaviors can result from negative thoughts

d. A structured, solution-based treatment

4. Interpersonal Theory

a. Theory predicated upon the individual's depression as a factor in an interpersonal setting

b. Also, one's depression can lead to problems in an interpersonal relationship

c. Treatment aimed at reducing symptoms, building self-esteem, and effective management of interpersonal and social relationships

F. Grief vs. Depression

1. Grief usually involves a measure of depression, but unlike serious mood disorder.

2. Serious depression involves consistent negativity in everyday functioning.

3. Serious depression may involve internally directed anger as well as severe insomnia.

4. Serious depression will find one's self-image as intrinsically worthless.

5. Serious depression is found when the individual is unresponsive to most normal stimuli and is anhedonic.

6. Serious depression is the root cause of suicidal ideation.

7. What is important to remember is that grief does not usually include serious clinical depression.

G. Dangers of Depression

1. Sense of happiness, well-being, "mental freedom" are gone.

2. Depression can threaten one's everyday life. Restlessness, sleeplessness, lack of pleasure, morbidity are present.

3. Employment, relationships, and health are jeopardized.

4. Sufferer may become suicidal.

H. Treatment of Depression

1. Psychotherapy

    a. Supportive Therapy

    b. Behavioral Therapy

    c. Cognitive Therapy

    d. Interpersonal Therapy

2. Chemotherapy (Pharmacological Intervention)

    a. Selective Serotonin-Reuptake Inhibitors (SSRIs), Zoloft, Prozac, Paxil and similar drug Effexor

3. Electroconvulsive Therapy (ECT) "Shock Treatment"

4. Depression-Recovery Model

Endnotes

[1] Eli Lilly and Co., *Simply live: A Guide to Your Recovery*, PW-22092 (Eli Lilly and Company, Indiana, 2001).

[2] Pfizer Inc., *Zoloft: for the Treatment of Depression*. 23-5712-00-2, TL565X99 (Pfizer; U.S. Pharmaceuticals, New York, 2000).

[3] John H. Greist, M.D. and James W. Jefferson, M.D., *Dealing with Depression: Taking Steps in the Right Direction* (Pfizer, U.S. Pharmaceuticals Group, New York, 1996).

[4] Pfizer, *supra* note 2; Greist, *supra* note 3.

[5] Lilly, *supra* note 1.

[6] *Diagnostic and Statistical Manual of Mental Disorders* 4th ed. (Washington, D.C.: American Psychiatric Association, 1994).

[7] *Id.*

[8] *Id.*

[9] *Id.*

[10] *Id.*, Martin B. Keller, George M. Simpson, Alan F. Schatzberg, and Myrna M. Weissman, *Learning to Live with Depression*, Medicine in the Public Interest, Inc. (MIPI) (Boston, 1994).

[11] Greist, *supra* note 3.

[12] Martin B. Keller, George M. Simpson, Alan F. Schatzberg, and Myrna M. Weissman, *Learning to Live with Depression*, Medicine in the Public Interest, Inc. (MIPI) (Boston, 1994); Greist, supra note 3.

[13] Keller, *supra* note 12.

[14] Keller, *supra* note 12; Greist, supra note 3.

[15] *Id.*

[16] Patrick M Del Zoppo, *Pastoral Bereavement Counseling: A Training Program for Caregivers in Ministry to the Bereaved* (New York: Archdiocese of New York, 1993).

[17] Charles H. Fishman, *Treating Troubled Adolescents: A Family Therapy Approach* (New York: Basic Books, Inc., 1988).

[18] *Id.*

[19] Burl E. Gilliland and Richard K. James, *Crisis Intervention Strategies* (California: Brooks/Cole, 1993).

[20] Keller *et al., supra* note 12.

[21] *Id.*

[22] *Id.*

[23] *Id.*

[24] *Id.*

[25] *Id.*

[26] *Id.*

[27] *Id.*

CHAPTER 8

Suicide

I. Introduction

Suicide among America's young people is an increasing concern. While statistics can fluctuate, it is sufficient to say that suicide among children and adolescents is significantly high.[1] It is interesting to note that while females are more prone to attempt suicide, males actually complete the act more often.[2] This can be accounted for, perhaps, by the greater propensity for males to use deadly firearms more frequently than females.[3] In addition, adolescent suicide is not restricted to children of lower-class problematic families. A new profile is surfacing that places adolescent suicide attemptors in a broad cross-section of socioeconomic variables.[4]

For our purposes, however, the question is not how many commit suicide, but rather why they do it. Albeit volumes have been written about this topic, the main purpose of this chapter is to briefly highlight some of the basic components that fit into the total picture.

II. Contributing Factors

A variety of factors can contribute to adolescent suicide. Certain psychological as well as social influences can propel a youngster toward self-destruction.

Some influences may be more obvious than others. For example, a youth who experienced the loss of a parent to suicide, or who has a borderline personality disorder, or who may be psychotic with little sense of structure or discipline may be susceptible to a self-destructive urge. Parental loss through abandonment, separation and divorce also are seen as contributing factors.[5]

Given the general emotional characteristics of the adolescent years, several additional factors, such as denial of reality, escape, hopelessness, anger, revenge, altruism, parental discord, parental pressures, substance abuse, school and social problems, helplessness, risk- taking, and inability to cope, all can play a significant role in the lethal process.[6] The key element common to all attempts at self-destruction is depression — an element that can be masked by other symptoms or problems.[7] Therefore, the school counselor would be well advised to carefully explore adolescent depression and not dismiss it as an age-specific phase or mood.

III. Types of Suicide

An important concept to bear in mind is that while, at times, it may be advantageous to classify behaviors by categories or syndromes, one must not do so with potential suicide victims. One cannot take the overall characteristics of adolescent behavior and apply them exactly in each individual case. Two fundamental concepts in suicide intervention are that (1) each individual potential suicide is a different situation; and (2) no matter how bizarre the circumstances, at that point in time the suicidal act makes sense to the victim.[8] There is, however, depression as a common element that can be of significance to the school counselor.[9]

In one expert's sociological approach to suicidal behavior, social influences are seen as significant determinants of such behavior.[10] Suicide can be divided into three classifications. The *egoistic suicide* is viewed as arising from the victim's failure to identify with or integrate into a particular group; the *anomic suicide* is seen as a result of the demise of societal norms, be it actual or perceived; and the *altruistic suicide* is linked to a sense of "social solidarity" for a worthy cause, perhaps the death will change things, for example, hara-kiri or self-immolation.[11] Given the general emotional characteristics of adolescence and the additional feelings associated with adolescent grief (see Chapter 6), it is not difficult to see the appropriateness of these classifications.

IV. Danger Signs

The questions now are: What does one look for? What are the signs? What does one do?

Inasmuch as depression is the common underlying variable, the prudent first-step would be to carefully explore a potential victim's behavior to determine if an underlying depression is, in fact, evident. The following list contains some guidelines used in assessing the presence of depression:

- depressed mood
- lack of interest or pleasure
- irritability
- behavioral changes
- loss of weight
- change in eating habits
- feelings of guilt
- lack of energy
- difficulty concentrating
- low self-esteem
- decline in school work
- sense of helplessness
- sadness
- sense of hopelessness
- change in sleep
- restlessness
- death-related thoughts
- suicidal thoughts

If a number of these signs are present for a period of time and constitute a difference in the student's ability to function, then a diagnosis of depression may be entertained and a referral to a professional therapist should be promptly made.[12]

V. Interventions

Once a student has, in fact, displayed significant signs of depression, the situation now becomes a matter of crisis intervention. The crisis interventionist or therapist will pursue a line of inquiry in an effort to determine the extent of lethality of the suicidal ideation.

In actual intervention, the therapist should pose some rather pointed questions in his or her assessment.

Have things been so bad that you've even thought about suicide? The therapist must be blunt and not skirt the issue. It is mythical that talking about suicide will actually give the individual the idea to do it. The therapist must evaluate certain risk factors (as previously mentioned), such as psychosis, substance abuse, depression, family history, formulating a plan, or giving away personal effects. When dealing with children, talking provides an alternative to acting and may actually lessen the risk of self-destruction.[13]

Have you ever thought about the act itself (i.e., formed a plan)? The therapist must know the extent of the plan and its degree of lethality — what method and its reversibility. Is it fast acting, tissue damaging (gunshot) or is it slow acting (pills, gas, cutting)?[14] If an individual appears to be at risk, then provisions must be made to remove the means of self-destruction from him or her.[15] One of the best tools for the interventionist to use is a reliable lethality scale (for example, Triage Assessment Form[16] or American Academy of Crisis

Interveners Lethality Scale).[17] If the lethality score is sufficiently high, then the therapist should move toward immediate referral for medical evaluation, observation, and possibly hospitalization.[18]

Are you currently taking medication? How much do you drink every day? No mention should be made of what the person drinks. One really wants to know if he or she is a substance abuser.

What would keep you from acting out your wish? The therapist should encourage the potential victim to consider what their friends would think and how their parents would react.

When actually involved in the tasks of intervention, the therapist must bear in mind that suicide is a cry for help. Most self-destructive individuals will exhibit some form of indication or "cries for help." No one is totally suicidal.[19]

Even people with strong self-destructive ideation usually have strong ambivalence about carrying out the act. Why then, if the desire to die is so great, would the person tell anyone about it? Why not just do it? There appears to be both a real death wish and confusion, a reaching out to be rescued. The ambivalent person lacks both logical thinking and a future perspective to envision a happier life. The counselor must be alert to this ambivalent behavior, for it easily can be misconstrued to be an insincere or false suicidal ideation. An understanding of this can put the suicidal person's behavior into the proper perspective. In the ambivalence, "[t]he suicidal person is looking for a rescuer to serve as an alter ego at a time when his own ego functions are severely impaired."[20] This is the optimum time for intervention — the therapist must act.

The therapist must recognize and highlight the ambivalence effectively. This is the therapist's "trump card" in dealing with the ambivalent client's confusion, diminished logic, and obscured options. Intervention looks for ambivalence. It is here that the therapist can "buy time" by using his or her own therapeutic optimism. He or she can ask the client to think it out, to "trust me."

The therapist must establish and use a therapeutic alliance (relationship). The therapist can make progress by assuring the client that he or she cares and is concerned. Specific statements such as, "Call me tomorrow at 10:00," are very useful.

Establish a "No Suicide Contract" with the person if the level of risk is not too high. The person must agree that if he or she can't keep the promise, then a call will be made to the therapist *immediately.* High-risk clients (with a high-lethality score) with no visible support system to keep vigil should be hospitalized immediately to ensure their safety. Confidentiality can be compromised to save a life.[21]

Help the client establish a linkage. The therapist must establish who is in the client's support system. Referrals to crisis groups and/or agencies also may be helpful. The therapist must help the client establish other linkages he or she must not be the client's sole support.

Help take the pressure off. The therapist should discuss the various stressors that the client is reacting to. Which is (are) the most burdensome? The therapist can help the client to decide what on the list can be removed.

Focus on the possibility of improvement. The therapist can use his or her therapeutic optimism to project better times ahead, resolution of problem(s), and a happier person, (especially when dealing with ambivalence).

The proper and careful assessment of the warning signs mentioned and the success of these six tasks can save a life.

VI. Survivor Reactions

In addition to facts, signs, and strategies, it is important to know what dynamics are in operation when a suicide has, in fact, occurred. Is the course of bereavement the same as with a natural death? What happens to the survivors?

When death has occurred by means of suicide, survivors will have essentially the same kinds of reactions they would have with any other mode of death. However, given the nature of the suicide event, the reactions will usually emerge with increased intensity. Certainly, shock and disbelief will be evident as will anger, resentment, and guilt.[22]

What exacerbates the pain and anguish is that suicidal death tends to turn survivors into "victims" also. The inordinate amount of anger and guilt that ensues, coupled with the societal stigmatization, place an enormous burden on the family and friends who are groping for the meaning of this death.[23] The awareness that the loved one willfully chose this mode of departure heightens resentment and feelings of rejection.[24]

Perhaps the most unnerving of all reactions is the incredible sense of survivor guilt that remains not only for being left behind, alive, but for not having been able to "read the signs" and possibly prevent the death. After all, suicide attempts are essentially a calling out for help. If the indications were picked up earlier, this tragedy might not have happened.[25]

In the school community it is extremely important to realize that most students will eventually heal and resume their normal lives. To do this, they must be provided with the necessary assistance and reassurance for them to realize that their discomfort will lessen with time. Students must be allowed to express their grief and school officials should be prepared to acknowledge and respect these feelings.[26]

In attempting to meet the needs of students after the death of a loved one, be it a contemporary or staff member, school officials should plan some form of memorialization. While this topic will be discussed more fully in Chapter 14, it merits mention at this point because a suicide death can present a unique problem with respect to inadvertently glorifying the deceased. Great care must be exercised so as to not encourage "copycat" or "cluster" suicides. While it is important to address the situation with factual information, it is best to do so without undue personal displays of emotion. The role of the school personnel is to recognize and acknowledge the mourners' pain and sorrow and to help ease the grief.[27] In the case of the altruistic suicide, undue glorification may equate the act to martyrdom and may even be appealing to other distressed students.

Research suggests that educational prevention programs, understanding adults and school officials, and school-based counseling and intervention programs are effective tools against this tragic loss of life.

VII. Summary

A. Background Facts

1. Suicide among young people a growing concern

2. More females attempt suicide

3. More males complete the act

4. Males more prone to use firearms

5. Adolescent suicides occur in families at all socio-economic levels.

B. Factors in Suicide of Young People

   1. Psychological factors

      a. Depression

      b. Borderline personality

      c. Psychosis

   2. Experience the loss of a parent to suicide

   3. Loss of parent through abandonment, separation, divorce

   4. Adolescent emotional characteristics can contribute

   5. Common element is depression

C. Fundamental Concepts for Intervention

   1. Each potential suicide is different

   2. Suicide makes sense to the victim

D. Types of Suicide

   1. Egoistic

   2. Anomic

   3. Altruistic

E. Danger Signs

   1. Depressed mood

   2. Sense of helplessness/hopelessness

   3. Death-related thoughts

   4. Suicidal thoughts

F. Interventions

   1. Counselor inquiry

   2. Lethality scale

3. Ambivalence

4. No suicide "contract"

5. Therapeutic alliance

G. Survivor Reactions

1. Social stigma

2. Anger/resentment

3. Guilt

4. Cluster suicides

H. Survivor Needs

1. Memorialization without glorification

2. Education, counseling, and intervention programs

Endnotes

[1] Patrick W. McKee, R. Wayne Jones, and Richard H. Barbe, *Suicide and the School: A Practical Guide to Suicide Prevention* (Pennsylvania: LRP Publications, 1993), 12; Laura Mufson, Donna Moreau, Myrna M. Weissman, and Gerald L. Klerman, *Interpersonal Psychotherapy for Depressed Adolescents* (New York: The Guilford Press, 1993), 162; Burl E. Gilliland, and Richard K. James, *Crisis Intervention Strategies* (California: Brooks/Cole, 1993), 130.

[2] Robin Lewis, Betty A. Walker, and Marilyn Mehr, "Counseling with Adolescent Suicidal Clients and Their Families," in *Crisis Intervention Handbook: Assessment, Treatment, and Research*, ed. A. Roberts (California: Wadsworth, Inc., 1990), 46.

[3] McKee, *supra* note 1, at 11-12.

[4] Lewis, *supra* note 2, at 46.

[5] Judith Marks Mishne, *Clinical Work with Adolescents* (New York: The Free Press, 1986), 207-08.

[6] *Id.* Frank J. Bruno, *Psychological Symptoms* (New York: John Wiley and Sons, Inc., 1993), 189; Lewis, *supra* note 2, at 46.

[7] Charles H. Fishman, *Treating Troubled Adolescents: A Family Therapy Approach* (New York: Basic Books, Inc., 1988), 159-60.

[8] Gilliland and James, *supra* note 1, at 130-131.

[9] Fishman, *supra* note 7.

[10] Gilliland and James, *supra* note 1.

[11] *Id.* at 130-31.

[12] *Diagnostic and Statistical Manual of Mental Disorders* 4th ed. (Washington, D.C.:American Psychiatric Association, 1994), 327; Harold L Kaplan, and Benjamin J. Sadock, *Pocket Handbook of Emergency Psychiatric Medicine* (Baltimore: Williams and Wilkins, 1993), 185; McKee, *supra* note 1, at 19-20.

[13] Jane E. Price, "The Effects of Divorce Precipitate a Suicide Threat" in *Play Therapy with Children in Crisis*, ed. N.B. Webb (New York: The Guilford Press, 1991), 205; Gilliland and James, *supra* note 1, at 132-33, 135.

[14] Price, *supra* note 13, at 206; Gilliland and James, *supra* note 1, at 135.

[15] Price, *supra* note 13, at 206.

[16] Gilliland and James, *supra* note 1, at 79-84, 135-36.

[17] James L. Greenstone and Sharon C. Leviton, *The Elements of Crisis Intervention* (California: Brooks/Cole, 1993), 19-20.

[18] Gilliland and James, *supra* note 1, at 136.

[19] *Id.* at 135.

[20] David J. Klugman, Robert E. Litman, and Carl I. Wold, "Suicide: Answering the Cry for Help," in *Differential Diagnosis and Treatment in Social Work*, ed. F. Turner (New York: The Free Press, 1983), 842.

[21] Gilliland and James, *supra* note 1, at 136, 150; Price, *supra* note 13, at 206.

[22] Martha D. Oates, *Death in the School Community. A Handbook for Counselors, Teachers, and Administrators* (Virginia: American Counseling Association, 1993), 55; Therese A. Rando, *Grief, Dying, and Death: Clinical Interventions for Caregivers* (Illinois: Research Press Co., 1984), 151.

[23] Rando, *supra* note 22, at 151; Gilliland and James, *supra* note 1, at 413.

[24] Rando, *supra* note 22, at 152; Gilliland and James, *supra* note 1, at 413.

[25] Rando, *supra* note 22, at 151-52; Gilliland and James, *supra* note 1, at 413; Oates, *supra* note 22, at 55.

[26] McKee, *supra* note 1, at 87-88.

[27] *Id.* at 84-85.

CHAPTER 9

Homicide and Traumatic Death

I. Introduction

In cases of sudden death, survivors are forced to confront the unexpected loss of someone dear to them without benefit of any preliminary warning.[1] The very suddenness of the event can precipitate its own set of problems. The survivor is deprived of his or her opportunity to say goodbye, or make certain plans, or tie up any loose ends. Loved ones are deprived of the chance to develop the necessary emotional preparations that will help them, later, to achieve a more viable grief resolution. The suddenness of the death event can actually foster a more prolonged grief journey.[2]

The net effect of a sudden death event is that it can leave the survivors in a state of shock, confusion, anxiety, and even depression. The rapidity of the death diminishes one's ability to adapt, to cope, and to function completely.[3] If the sudden death involves a suicide, survivors also may find themselves overwhelmed with bouts of irrational guilt and self-reproach. Family and friends may needlessly assume the blame for not having detected a problem, for not having "seen the signs." They may see themselves as being responsible for an event that they might have prevented.[4]

A homicide death, like death by suicide or accident, is usually a sudden event that occurs unannounced.[5] By virtue of its abruptness, the event evokes not only the negative emotional reactions that normally result an act of violence, but also all the reactions pertinent to its suddenness. It is important to understand these reactions as well as the resultant behavior(s).

The common denominator of sudden death events is that the survivors are left stunned, surprised, and cheated of the opportunity to adequately take leave of their loved one. They have difficulty understanding the loss and are left to ruminate over the details in an effort to make sense out of what has happened.[6] The intent of this chapter is to focus on one specific type of sudden death — the homicide.

In an increasingly more violent society, homicide is a common cause of death, especially among the economically disadvantaged and

119

among people of color.[7] Oddly enough, the American judicial process has coined a new definition of homicide. In some venues, the removal of certain life-support systems may, in fact, legally constitute an act of homicide. It could be considered "active euthanasia."[8] The major distinction in this case is that the death is neither sudden nor violent. Although genuine grief will be felt and must be resolved, the negative reactions that usually accompany the sudden and violent homicide will not be in evidence and grief resolution should not be unnecessarily prolonged.

II. Grief Reactions to Homicide

In addition to the reactions that accompany a sudden death, in general, the homicide of an adolescent will produce many painful and provocative reactions that will make grief resolution a precarious journey. Parents will experience a unique and idiosyncratic grief (see Chapter 2) fraught with feelings of consuming rage, helplessness, and perhaps even self-reproach. The victim's family may yearn for vengeance and punishment and, later, justice.[9] However, even in justice there is pain. If and when the perpetrator is arrested, tried, and convicted, the survivors will relive the feelings of shock and anger; much of the pain will be "reawakened."[10] Therefore, closure to the resolution of grief will be unduly prolonged.

When confronting a homicide death, survivors are forced to agonize over the senselessness of the act. This death could have been prevented, it was unnecessary, and it was the arbitrary act of someone who deliberately deprived them of their loved one. Some survivors may even experience feelings of guilt over possibilities that they somehow could have prevented the murder.[11]

Family and friends must begin to work through their feelings of rage, guilt, and sense of impotence caused by this horrendous act of violence.[12] This will take time and is often complicated by another factor unique to this kind of death — the criminal justice system.

Many aspects of the system can complicate the mourning process by the sheer frustration they cause: no arrests have been made, lack of information from the police, plea bargaining, the killer free on bail, evidence being thrown out of court, lenient sentences, and the murderer being given an early parole. Sometimes it may even appear that the victim and/or the family are being "lost" in the process. Survivors of homicide deaths may feel that they are being victimized a second time by the system and, perhaps, even by the media. All possible situations place added stress on the grieving process.[13] Part of this added stress also can be attributed to exhaustive financial burdens, such as the funeral, medical (psychiatric) expenses, and possible costs for private lawyers and/or investigators. The counselor should make survivors aware of these possibilities so they can be prepared to deal with them. There often is a correlation between the resolution of grief and the resolution of these other matters.[14]

A. Posttraumatic Stress Disorder

One of the factors related to homicide which, most certainly, affects the course of grief resolution is the trauma that attends the death event,[15] especially if the survivor is an actual witness to the violence. The contemporary concept of trauma has evolved to go beyond any single event to encompass a continuous or cumulative experience. Those who experience trauma are perceived to have experienced inordinate events or actions that may leave them "psychologically numb and emotionally anesthetized."[16] These people can be considered "victims" of the crime as well. They may suffer flashbacks of the violence, insomnia, and other experiences that will be described shortly. It is important to note that the purpose of this chapter is to provide some factual material relevant to homicidal death events and possible treatment options merely to assist the counselor in the areas of possible diagnosis and referral. The school bereavement counselor ordinarily should not initiate treatment. This condition, known as posttraumatic stress disorder (PTSD), *must* be treated by an experienced mental health professional.

Homicide survivors may exhibit a bereavement that may have a pathological appearance, and these individuals will require interventions for "both PTSD and complicated mourning."[17]

The following lists indicate some of the characteristic symptoms that might indicate the presence of PTSD. Again, these are given for the purposes of *diagnosis* and *referral*.

Some of the Symptoms of PTSD
- Disturbances in sleep, nightmares, recurring dreams
- Reliving of traumatic event, flashbacks, bad memories

- Anxiety, irritability, emotional withdrawal
- Fear of strangers, detachment from others
- Eating disturbances, survivor guilt, excessive alertness
- Apprehensive of recurring trauma, relationship problems
- Avoidance of memory arousing activities
- Outbursts of anger, rage[18]

Some Alternative Symptoms in Children

- Obscure, yet frightening dreams
- Anger, agitated or belligerent behavior
- Traumatic themes expressed in play
- School phobias, depression, sadness[19]

Some Additional Symptoms in Adolescents

- Apathy, loss of interest in environmental activities
- Altered personality
- Anxiety
- Acting out
- Suicidal ideation[20]

The treatment of PTSD is a very delicate prospect and requires expert professional training. There are additional circumstances or behaviors ("masked presentations") that may be related to PTSD[21] as well as preexisting psychopathology[22] or other significant coexisting problems.[23] For these reasons, the school bereavement counselor is well advised to make the necessary referrals for appropriate professional intervention.

When trauma survivors are mourning, they must be helped to identify and seek resolution of all losses. One expert perceives the grief process as consisting of a three-level series of these losses.[24] Level one relates to certain "tangible losses" such as the death of a loved one or the loss of a body part or a home. Certain "intangible losses" such as feelings, concepts, and trust also can be included at this level. The next level deals with a sense of powerlessness that results from the loss of personal dignity and innocence or the loss of social, vocational, and even certain romantic opportunities as direct results of the traumatic experience. These losses also must be identified and grieved. The final level deals with the confrontation of the survivor's own mortality. In all turmoil, pain, and sorrow, the survivor will, at one point, come to realize that he or she is not immortal. Thus, one's own mortality will be grieved as well. This realization is inevitable when one grieves the death of another. This mortality can be viewed as "the ultimate expression of powerlessness."[25]

Three principal conditions can precipitate posttraumatic reactions during mourning.[26] In a "personal encounter with death" the individual experiences feelings of abandonment, anxiety, terror, helplessness, fear, and vulnerability. The individual seeks "relief and rescue." This condition could occur during a mugging or auto accident in which the survivor is left alive and basically unharmed.[27] The second condition deals with the survivor's "massive, shocking, and sudden confrontation with the death and mutilation of others."[28] These experiences may occur within the mishaps of war or through natural or vehicular disasters. The survivor in these circumstances also is vulnerable to fear, terror, a sense of helplessness, and to the emergence of posttraumatic stress.[29] The third condition relates to the "confrontation with the traumatic and/or mutilating death of a loved one." This experience can arise when one comes upon the body of a loved one who has committed suicide, or when a survivor must identify the charred and mutilated body of a son or daughter, or even when an accident survivor awakes to find the mangled body of a loved one next to him. While these incidents will cause the survivor to reflect on his or her own mortality, the person is not in any imminent danger at the moment of discovery or confrontation. Yet, the same reactions of fear, helplessness, terror, vulnerability, arousal, shock, and anxiety will prevail.[30]

At this point, it should be abundantly clear that a death by homicide, or other similarly violent means, has the very real potential of thrusting survivors into complicated mourning and posttraumatic stress disorder. Consequently, the survivors must be treated with care and skill by competent personnel. It is a lengthy and tedious process that would be more efficacious outside the school environment. Knowledgeable school counselors can be of invaluable service in the timely identification, diagnosis, and referral of these suffering individuals.

III. Summary

A. Similarities Between Homicide and Sudden Death

1. Death is rapid and unexpected

2. No time for unfinished business

3. No time to adequately take leave of the loved one

4. Survivor(s) may be left in state of shock, confusion, even depression

5. Suddenness of death event can diminish survivors' ability to adapt, cope, and function

B. Homicide

1. Demographics

2. Legalities

3. Painful and provocative reactions

   a. Feelings of rage, helplessness, self-reproach

   b. Agony over senselessness of the act; death was unnecessary, preventable

   c. Desire for vengeance, punishment, justice

   d. Risk of pain being "reawakened"

   e. Grief resolution may be prolonged

C. Frustration with the System

1. Lack of information

2. Lack of arrest(s)

3. Perpetrator out on bail

4. Plea bargaining

5. Evidence rejected by court

6. Lenient sentences and early parole

D. Financial Burden

1. Victim's medical and funeral expenses

2. Survivors' psychotherapeutic expenses

3. Possible costs for private lawyers/investigators

E. Survivors' Trauma

1. Shock, confusion, anxiety

2. Guilt, self-reproach

3. Posttraumatic Stress Disorder

    a. Should be diagnosed and referred to experienced professional for treatment

    b. May go beyond single episode experience

    c. Flashbacks, insomnia, anger, anxiety, and other symptoms

    d. Tri-level series of losses

    e. Precipitants of PTSD

    f. Admonitions for treatment

Endnotes

[1] Mary Elizabeth Mancini, "Creating and Therapeutically Utilizing Anticipatory Grief in Survivors of Sudden Death" T. Rando (ed.), *Loss and Anticipatory Grief*, ed. T. Rando (Massachusetts: D.C. Heath and Co., 1986), 145-52.

[2] Carel B. Germain, *Human Behavior in the Social Environment* (New York: Columbia University Press, 1991), 386; Therese A. Rando, *How to Go on Living When Someone You Love Dies* (New York: Bantam Books, 1991), 90, 110.

[3] Rando, *supra* note 2, at 90.

[4] Germain, *supra* note 2, at 387.

[5] *Id.* at 386.

[6] Rando, *supra* note 2, at 91.

[7] Judson R. Landis, *Sociology: Concepts and Characteristics* (8th ed.) (California: Wadsworth Inc., 1992), 156, 188, 191.

[8] Dennis A. Robbins, "Legal and Ethical Issues in Terminal Illness Care for Patients, Families, Caregivers, and Institutions," *Loss and Anticipatory Grief*, ed. T. Rando (Massachusetts: D.C. Heath and Co., 1986), 215-28.

[9] Germain, *supra* note 2, at 387.

[10] *Id.*

[11] Rando, *supra* note 2, at 110.

[12] Germain, *supra* note 2, at 387; Rando, *supra* note 2, at 110.

[13] Rando, *supra* note 2, at 111.

[14] *Id.*

[15] Therese A. Rando, *Treatment of Complicated Mourning* (Illinois: Research Press Co., 1993), 7.

[16] Bert Kaplan, "Anxiety States" in *Adult Psychopathology: A Social Work Perspective*, ed. F.J. Turner (NewYork: The Free Press, 1984), 260-279.

[17] Rando, *supra* note 15, at 537.

[18] *Diagnostic and Statistical Manual of Mental Disorders* (4th ed.) (Washington, D.C.: American Psychiatric Association, 1994), 428; Aphrodite Matsakis, *Posttraumatic Stress Disorder: A Complete Treatment Guide* (California: New Harbinger Publications, Inc., 1994), 19; Rando, *supra* note 15, at 537.

[19] *Diagnostic and Statistical Manual, supra* note 18, at 428; Burl E. Gilliland, and Richard K. James; *Crisis Intervention Strategies* (California: Brooks/Cole, 1993), 181.

[20] Matsakis, *supra* note 18, at 19; Gilliland and James, *supra* note 19, at 181.

[21] Matsakis, *supra* note 18, at 20-21.

[22] Gilliland and James, *supra* note 19, at 167-68.

[23] Matsakis, *supra* note 18, at 99-100.

[24] *Id.*

[25] *Id.* at 258, 260-61.

[26] Rando, *supra* note 15.

[27] *Id.* at 578.

[28] *Id.*

[29] *Id.* at 579.

[30] *Id.* at 580.

CHAPTER 10

Terrorism

I. Introduction

Sept. 11, 2001—Not since Dec. 7, 1941, has an act of enemy destruction caused America to reel in such horror. The destruction of the twin towers of the World Trade Center in the heart of downtown Manhattan was so unexpected, so sudden and so utterly horrific that the entire free world was moved to tears. The damage and carnage defied belief. Perhaps, never before was death and destruction so complete.

The most appallingly distinctive aspect of this tragedy was that there was no national perpetrator, no surrounding army, no nuclear holocaust. It was a coldly calculated act to strike terror into the hearts of a free people. A terror that still lingers months later.

II. Terrorism

Terrorism, the violent act to instill terror, is the newest and, perhaps, most morally damaging weapon in the arsenal of those who seek to fragment the ever-delicate status of world peace. The suddenness, the horror, the deception, and the shock only further exacerbate the already difficult task of grieving a loss. The proverbial "Pandora's box" of frightening emotions is cast wide open.

This chapter will help identify the various emotions that come into play and negotiate the dangers and pitfalls along the circuitous road to recovery. Areas such as vulnerability, insecurity, depression, anger, guilt, and a host of accompanying variations and complications will be discussed.

While some of these factors may not be "new" to the reader, the fact remains that there are new complications that have emerged for the first time. New considerations and new challenges have surfaced, making the need for bereavement knowledge much more critical.

Perhaps the singularly most unique and debilitating element that arose from this tragic blot on human decency was the incredible sense of gross vulnerability that Americans were left with. Up to this point, war, attacks and danger were all far away. Americans went to bed at night without the fear of imminent danger. On Sept. 11, 2001, the picture radically changed. America was attacked on her own soil with her own equipment.

Since the end of the Cold War and its daily potential for nuclear disaster, Americans have led fairly blissful lives with the usual humdrum assortment of worries. Of course, there were sporadic and cyclical concerns such as the economy, unemployment and events such as Granada, Chernobyl and foreign viruses. However, there was a feeling of security rooted in the firm belief that just about anything could be achieved — even cures for cancer and AIDS — if we put our minds to it. It was more a question of priority than possibility (Malcolm, 2001-2002 pp. 31-32).[1] There was an air of security and optimism. Americans were more or less content. However, not for too long. Andrew Malcolm, in *Thunder Across the Land* (Malcolm, p. 32),[2] poignantly describes another "Shot heard 'round the world" that occurred on that fateful day in September.

> And then in an instant before our disbelieving eyes, up in those same sudden pillars of dirty smoke, went an invisible panoply of shared certainties and assumptions. Suddenly, a toxic combination of events shattered our territorial invulnerability, probably forever.

(Malcolm, p. 32)[3]

The operant word here is *vulnerable*. America was laid emotionally open, momentarily helpless and defenseless to assault. Webster (p. 1604) defines *vulnerable* as, "that which can be wounded or physically injured, open to criticism or attack; easily hurt."[4] In truth, "[a] level of American innocence was also incinerated in those fires." (Malcolm, p. 33).[5]

The terrorists, being too few in number and too suicidal in nature to prevail, correctly calculated that this would be the American weakness. They knew, full well, that they needed our unsuspecting and illicit cooperation in order to succeed. "Terrorists cannot win without our acquiescence in falling victim to the invisible, deadly spores of fear. So we are invisibly invited to become complicit in their conspiracy against ourselves." (Malcolm, p. 34)[6]

When death occurs within the parameters just described, the grief resolution journey is not significantly changed. It can become, however, greatly intensified and much more complicated. Most death events will tend to leave survivors with a sense of being vulnerable, and depression certainly plays a part. When death follows an act of terrorism, it is here that the author feels that one's vulnerability is fully realized and depression becomes most acute as with Kübler-Ross's dying patients (1969).[7] The final step is acceptance, but the problem is that it emerges as a dichotomy. In Chapter 4, the reader saw the need for acceptance as a necessary, "Task of Grief." However, Ross's acceptance referred to the vulnerability of life and the depression attendant to the decedent him/herself. The post-terrorism dichotomy presents the survivor with the additional prospect of accepting his/her own vulnerability and depression as well. This appears to be more devastating than any one conventional, singular death event. So devastating, in fact, that the writer would be remiss not to reiterate the concept of initial shock previously described in Chapter 1. Here, shock is seen as nature's innate form of anesthesia that tends to control how much reality one can absorb at any one given time. It serves as nature's own emotional "buffer." The woman mentioned in Chapter 2, actually described the shock that she experienced as a "little gift" that sustained her when confronted with something that she could not possibly have fully realized (Del Zoppo 1989, p. 6).[8]

At this point, it would be incumbent upon the reader to begin to carefully consider the emotional ramifications resulting from a terrorist attack, namely: depression, anger, and guilt. On September 11, 2001, Americans were introduced to these emotions in their most gripping forms.

III. Attendant Depression

As discussed in Chapter 7, depression is a term that is widely used today with variant meanings. In this chapter, the writer will provide a functional, everyday understanding of the term. (A more inclusive and, perhaps, more clinical narrative is given in Chapter 7, "Depression.")

With one out of every eight Americans, or 12.5 percent, experiencing some form of depression in the course of their lifetime (Lilly 2001, p.15),[9] depression is not an uncommon condition. (See Chapter 7). Although already listed in Chapter 8, some of the salient symptoms will be repeated here for convenience.

- depressed mood
- lack of interest or pleasure
- irritability
- behavioral changes
- loss of weight
- change in eating habits
- feelings of guilt
- lack of energy
- difficulty concentrating
- low self-esteem
- decline in school work
- sense of helplessness
- sadness
- sense of hopelessness
- change in sleep
- restlessness
- death-related thoughts
- suicidal thoughts

(*Diagnostic and Statistical Manual of Mental Disorders*, 4th ed. 1994, p. 327).[10]

As a result of the horror, destruction and loss of September 11, 2001, many Americans have begun to suffer varying degrees of these symptoms. Some, as indicated, will pass with time, others, however, will linger and necessitate professional intervention. The most important factor is that the counselor, caretakers, and friends of the troubled individual(s) recognize the symptoms and encourage them to seek professional help. Sufferers should *not* try to go it alone.

The most important concept to remember is that one need not always have to be a trained professional to help. Part of the overall picture, as seen in the chapter on suicide, are those individuals, family and friends who make up the depressed person's support system. The value of this support system, or "team" cannot be overstated. Often, it is these caring individuals who not only recognize and understand the symptoms, but who can actually monitor the sufferer in daily life and can suggest treatment and even prevent harm.

The net result of that fateful day is that all Americans were shocked into an awareness of what terrorism really entailed and were all affected by its horror and demoralization. It is out of the massive loss of life, property, security, and feeling of vulnerability that the seeds of depression are sewn.

IV. Anger

Anger is a phenomenon that has merited attention throughout the ages in social settings, literature, and even in scriptures. It has been both condemned and praised as being destructive, on one hand, and beneficial on the other (McKay et al. 1989, p. 9).[11] It is somewhat safe to assume that there are both myths and realities attributed to this stormy emotion.

McKay et al. (pp. 9-10)[12] delineate four basic myths about anger that are currently being considered. These writers contend that anger is: (1) biochemical in nature; (2) anger is an instinct in man; (3) anger and frustration can yield to aggression; and (4) anger can be seen as a positive means of ventilation.

As interesting as these theories may be, they are offered as background information only. They are not germane to the purpose here. What one must remember are the realities that are known about anger and how they impact upon the lives of the survivors of tragic events. A more in-depth treatment of this topic can be found in Chapter 11, "The Role of Anger." However, for the convenience of the reader, salient aspects will be repeated here.

As indicated in an earlier chapter, survivors must realize that anger can result from feelings toward the lost loved one as well as at the reason or way the death occurred (Rando 1993, pp. 467-68).[13] In the particular case of the terrorist attack of September 11, 2001, the writer strongly suspects the latter reason as the principal cause. It is important to further note that, in addition to feelings of rage, anger also can become entwined in the survivor's defense mechanisms. Anger can serve to mask other emotions such as depression, guilt, anxiety, loss, and frustration (Rando 1993, pp. 467-68) (McKay et al. 1989, pp. 218-20).[14]

Consequently, anger should not be taken lightly or summarily. Of course, it is obvious that the survivor would be angry at the actual death and the mode of death. However, the prudent counselor would be wise to pursue the angry feelings in an effort to unmask additional feelings, if any, that the survivor may be hiding or actually "blocking." A failure to do so could actually keep the sufferer from addressing the issue(s) that produced the feelings initially (McKay et al. 1989, p. 221).[15]

V. Guilt

Another phenomenon that impacts the survivor's quality of grief resolution is the possible appearance of strong feelings of guilt. While these feelings are largely without actual basis, they have the potential to seriously impede the survivor's journey toward healing (Worden

1982, p. 42).[16] The reader is directed to a fuller discussion of this phenomenon presented in Chapter 12, "The Role of Guilt."

For the purposes of this discussion, the writer will present some of the more salient aspects of understanding guilt in an effort to better provide the reader/counselor with a realistic grasp of the nature of this particular feeling.

As indicated in an earlier chapter, there are three basic types of guilt that warrant attention in this treatment of the death event.

Survivor's Guilt. Essentially, this form of guilt may emerge when one individual has survived a death event in which another individual did not. There may be feelings of powerlessness at not having been able to prevent the loss. Survivors may feel culpable, perhaps even that they might have been able to prevent the loss but didn't. They may even experience a "secret" relief that they survived the event (Rando 1993, p. 481).[17]

Functional Guilt. Sometimes guilt may serve a "protective function" by masking other anxiety-producing feelings that the survivor may wish to avoid. A classic example is a feeling of guilt that is so strong that it completely overshadows the survivor's unwillingness to say goodbye, i.e., the "function" of the guilt was to save the survivor the rigors of separation-anxiety. There may, of course, be other crucial issues as well. The net result is that there is no validity to the guilt, per se. Essentially, it was created for a purpose, and its treatment should not be taken lightly and should be undertaken by a skilled professional (Rando 1993, p. 483).[18]

Contributory Guilt. A form of self-reproach, contributory guilt causes the survivor to believe that he/she may have actually contributed to their loved one's demise (Rando 1993, p. 481).[19] Take, for example, the following hypothetical scenario: A husband awakes on the morning of September 11, 2001 with a stuffy nose and a cough. He decides to stay at home and not report to work at the Twin Towers. His wife, thinking his illness minor, encourages him to go to work. Perhaps two hours later, the terrorists strike the buildings, and the husband perishes in the aftermath. The grief-stricken wife now reproaches herself relentlessly. "If I had only let him stay at home, he would be alive now. It's my fault that he is dead." It is abundantly obvious that his wife had absolutely nothing to do with his death. However, she is inconsolable in her grief. The husband's death, itself, has produced enough pain. She should not have to endure more unnecessarily. This scenario demands the intervention of a highly trained mental health professional for adequate resolution.

There may be times when a valid guilt may emerge. Only trained practitioners should intervene using techniques as the "empty chair" exercises that permit verbalization of feelings, "forgiveness" exercises, cemetery visitations, and follow-up processing. This form of counseling must not be attempted by laymen (Jongsma and Peterson 1995, pp. 70-71).[20]

VI. Posttraumatic Stress Disorder

When death occurs as a result of tragedy or violence, there may be an additional area to be considered or explored. It is not a feeling like anger, guilt, or depression, but rather a kind of haunting psychological state. Our contemporary concept of trauma has evolved to go beyond any one, single event to encompass a continuous or cumulative experience. Those who have experienced trauma are perceived to have experienced inordinate events or actions that may leave them, "psychologically numb and emotionally anesthetized." The survivors may suffer flashbacks of the trauma, insomnia, and a host of other symptoms that will be noted shortly (Kaplan 1984, pp. 260-279).[21] This condition came to be known as Posttraumatic Stress Disorder (PTSD). It is a complex phenomenon that was originally dubbed "shell shock" in bygone war years. There is, however, a caveat. The neophyte counselor should be familiar with enough symptoms to enable a diagnosis but, ordinarily, should not initiate treatment. This, again, must be done only by an experienced practitioner. The treatment of PTSD is a very delicate prospect and requires expert professional training.

The writer's purpose in this work is merely to state some of the characteristic symptoms that might indicate the presence of PTSD. These are given for the purpose of diagnosis and referral only. The reader is strongly encouraged to read more about the complexities of PTSD in Chapter 9, "Homicide and Traumatic Death."

Some of the Symptoms of PTSD

- Disturbances in sleep, nightmares, recurring dreams
- Reliving of traumatic event, flashbacks, bad memories
- Anxiety, irritability, emotional withdrawal
- Fear of strangers, detachment from others
- Eating disturbances, survivor guilt, excessive alertness
- Apprehensive of recurring trauma, relationship problems
- Avoidance of memory arousing activities
- Outbursts of anger, rage

(*Diagnostic and Statistical Manual*, 1994, p. 428) (Matsakis 1994, p. 19) (Rando 1993, p. 7).[22]

Some Alternative Symptoms in Children

- Obscure, yet frightening dreams
- Anger, agitated or belligerent behavior
- Traumatic themes expressed in play
- School phobias, depression, sadness

(*Diagnostic and Statistical Manual*, 1994, p. 428) (Gilliland and James 1993, p. 181).[23]

Some Additional Symptoms in Adolescents

- Apathy, loss of interest in environmental activities
- Altered personality
- Anxiety
- Acting out
- Suicidal ideation

(Matsakis 1994, p. 19) (Gilliland and James 1993, p. 181)[24]

VII. Summary

A. Terrorism

    1. A violent act to instill fear

    2. Gives rise to vulnerability, insecurity, depression, anger, guilt, and fear

    3. New challenges

    4. Territorial invulnerability shattered

    5. Feelings of helplessness and defenselessness

    6. Feeling of innocence destroyed

    7. Shock and disbelief

B. Depression

    1. Long lasting

    2. Affects thinking, bodily functioning, and behavior

    3. Depressed mood, lack of interest or pleasure, low self-esteem, change in eating habits, weight loss, suicidal ideation, sense of difficulty concentrating, hopelessness, etc.

    4. Support system

    5. Seek treatment — don't go it alone

C. Anger

    1. Instinctive in man

    2. May lead to aggression

    3. May be viewed as a means of ventilation

    4. May be directed at a loved one as well as at an enemy

    5. Anger can mask other emotions such as guilt, anxiety, loss, etc.

D. Guilt

    1. Most post-death guilt is without basis

2. Survivor guilt

3. Functional guilt

4. Contributory guilt

5. Occasional valid guilt

6. Intervention by qualified mental health practitioner

E. Posttraumatic Stress Disorder (PTSD)

1. A "haunting" psychological state

2. May go beyond single-episode experience

3. Flashbacks, insomnia, anger, anxiety, and other symptoms

4. Should be referred to experienced professional for treatment

Endnotes

[1] Andrew H. Malcolm, *Thunder Across the Land*, "Notre Dame Magazine," Indiana, Vol. 30, No. 4, Winter 2001-02.

[2] *Id.*

[3] *Id.*

[4] *Webster's New World College Dictionary*, Fourth Edition, ©2000, 1999 by IDG Books Worldwide, Inc., California.

[5] Malcolm, *supra* note 1.

[6] *Id.*

[7] Elisabeth Kübler-Ross, *On Death and Dying* (New York: Macmillan Publishing Co., 1969).

[8] Patrick M. Del Zoppo, *To Be Lifted Up: The Journey from Grief to Healing* (New York: Archdiocese of New York, 1989).

[9] Eli Lilly and Co., *Simply live: A Guide to Your Recovery*, PW-22092 (Eli Lilly and Company, Indiana, 2001).

[10] *Diagnostic and Statistical Manual of Mental Disorders* 4th ed. (Washington, D.C.: American Psychiatric Association, 1994).

[11] Matthew McKay, Peter D. Rogers, and Judith McKay, *When Anger Hurts: Quieting the Storm Within* (California: New Harbinger Publications, Inc., 1989).

[12] *Id.*

[13] Therese A. Rando, *Treatment of Complicated Mourning* (Illinois: Research Press Co., 1993).

[14] *Id.*, McKay, *supra* note 11.

[15] McKay, *supra* note 11.

[16] J. William Worden, *Grief Counseling and Grief Therapy: A Handbook for the Mental Health Practitioner* (New York: Springer Publishing Co., 1982).

[17] Rando, *supra* note 13.

[18] *Id.*

[19] *Id.*

[20] Arthur E. Jongsma, Jr. and L. Mark Peterson, *The Complete Psychotherapy Treatment Planner* (New York: John Wiley and Sons, Inc., 1995).

[21] Bert Kaplan, "Anxiety States." In *Adult Psychopathology: A Social Work Perspective*, edited by F.J. Turner (NewYork: The Free Press, 1984).

[22] *Diagnostic and Statistical Manual of Mental Disorders* 4th ed. (Washington, D.C.: American Psychiatric Association, 1994); Aphrodite Matsakis, *Post-Traumatic Stress Disorder: A Complete Treatment Guide* (California: New Harbinger Publications, Inc., 1994); Therese A. Rando, *Treatment of Complicated Mourning* (Illinois: Research Press Co., 1993).

[23] *Diagnostic and Statistical Manual of Mental Disorders* 4th ed. (Washington, D.C.: American Psychiatric Association, 1994); Burl E. Gilliland and Richard K. James, *Crisis Intervention Strategies* (California: Brooks/Cole, 1993).

[24] Aphrodite Matsakis, *Post-Traumatic Stress Disorder: A Complete Treatment Guide* (California: New Harbinger Publications, Inc., 1994); Burl E. Gilliland and Richard K. James, *Crisis Intervention Strategies* (California: Brooks/Cole, 1993).

CHAPTER 11

The Role of Anger

I. Introduction

One can hardly entertain a discussion about death and anger without deferring to the monumental contribution made by the eminent physician and thanatologist, Dr. Elisabeth Kübler-Ross. In *On Death and Dying*,[1] Dr. Kübler-Ross describes and clarifies the roles and functions that anger can accomplish in matters related to the death event. While her observations were primarily concerned with the loved one who was dying, the reactions observed were not incongruent with what is experienced by those left behind.

II. Anger as a Reaction

Anger can be seen as a reaction that is difficult to deal with, since it may lash out at any time and in any direction. Nothing can please or soothe the one who is angry; almost anything and anyone are bound to cause displeasure. Negative reactions to the suffering person's attitude only promote the rage and discomfort.[2] Anger may be used to foster one's memory as well as to assert oneself. It is a way of saying, "I'm alive, don't forget that."[3]

The unfortunate result is that caregivers and family frequently respond with a subjective anger of their own, which only complements the loved one's unique hostility. Ultimately, needless arguments and avoidance behaviors may ensue.[4] Anger can be counterproductive and even destructive; a greater understanding of anger can avoid unnecessary turmoil.

Another aspect of pre-death anger is the functional role that it can play. Ross cites an example of how a patient fostered an ambiance of loneliness and avoidance in order to protect herself from thinking about the proximity of her own impending death.[5] Issues of fear and separation anxiety can be comfortably put aside while neatly camouflaged by this functional anger.

141

III. Survivor Resolution of Anger

Survivors should be made aware of the nature and purpose of such hostile behavior. It may help them to develop an awareness of their own coping mechanisms as well as to understand the patient's feelings. Through these actions, survivors can help the patient gain relief as he or she struggles with trying to accept the ultimate finality of his or her own earthly existence.[6]

This stage can be described as having a "why me?" configuration, in which the patient can no longer exist in the denial mode and reacts to the realization of impending death with not only anger, but also with resentment, rage, and even hostility. This may be viewed as the patient's desperate need for attention, to exert some modicum of control, and to muster understanding and, perhaps, even respect.[7]

Once the loved one has, in fact, passed away, the role of anger is not yet completed. The survivors must now confront and resolve their own issues in this area. Anger is a common post-loss experience and a potential source of problems and confusion.[8]

Survivors may frequently find themselves angry at the deceased for having left them. They may experience great frustration at not having been able to forestall the death event. The death may even precipitate what one expert calls a "regressive experience." This experience is a kind of reliving of the separation anxiety felt in childhood when one momentarily loses contact with a parent while shopping. The regression frequently may occur with the death of a significant person in the survivor's cycle of life. It can produce an anger born out of one's anxiety over feelings of inability to continue in the loved one's absence. These feelings must be qualified and accordingly directed toward the loved one in order to facilitate meaningful grief resolution.[9] The author is vividly reminded of the widow who slapped her deceased husband as he lay in the casket "for having died on her." While this behavior is not common, anger, nevertheless, may be present.

At times, death-related anger is poorly managed and may be channeled toward another living person who may then be blamed for the death. With this mind set, "[i]f someone can be blamed, then he is responsible and, hence, the loss could have been prevented."[10] The number of post-death family feuds and malpractice suits may be linked to this phenomenon. In extreme cases, the anger may be directed inwardly, against oneself and, in cases of depression, may precipitate a suicidal ideation.[11]

Anger can be viewed as an anticipated reaction to be seen in the aftermath of losing a significant loved one.[12] It is not an unnatural result of having someone of value taken away; yet societal attitudes are not conducive to this expression of anger. There is little deference given to "acknowledgment and coping" with respect to such a normal emotion.[13]

Anger may be generated not only by the deceased for having left the survivor to "carry on alone,"[14] but also by something that the loved one may or may not have done while still alive.[15] The acknowledgment of this form of anger is problematic in that societal norms tend to frown upon blaming or making negative remarks about the dead.[16]

Often, anger may be unconsciously directed or displaced onto other people. It is possible for anger to be expressed toward doctors or innocent people who may not have sustained such a loss, or even toward God. The survivors also may express anger toward themselves through feelings of guilt, lack of worth, or even personal hatred. Behaviors of self-punishment and even self-destruction may not be uncommon. What is important for survivor growth and grief resolution is for those left behind to identify and validate their feelings. They must realize that they have a right to the feelings that surface and must begin to channel these feelings in appropriate and acceptable ways.[17]

IV. Reasons Anger Arises

Survivors must come to the realization that anger can result for more than one reason.[18] Anger can result from feelings toward the loved one as well as at the reason or way the death occurred. The important thing to realize is that these angry feelings can often disguise other emotions such as feelings of depression, anxiousness, or even a sense of survivor dependency. In such a setting, the survivor must be helped to gently identify and understand the possible causes of the perceived anger. Once the mourner has acknowledged that he or she does, in fact, experience such feelings, the counselor should try to help the individual label (identify) the feelings and attempt to trace them. The survivor should seek means of expression in an effort to work through whatever may be camouflaged by the angry feelings. He or she must be allowed to ventilate the anger as well as to re-channel these feelings in meaningful and acceptable ways. The survivor must be made to realize that one person's anger may potentially have a causal effect on another individual's or a group's expression of emotion(s).[19]

Anger can play the role of defense mechanism.[20] Anger can be used to protect against guilt, anxiety, loss, fear, unworthiness, and frustration.[21] The nature of anger has been described as "addictive" in that it is something that has been learned to defend an individual from some of these negative feelings. As an addiction, anger can be used to "block" discomfort while providing a brief measure of "control" and moments of "well-being."[22]

An individual's anger can be an obstacle to confronting one's loss.[23] It is seen as impeding the grieving process, preventing the mourner from "letting go," and, in essence, can set the stage for unresolved grief. People with anger may not be able to relate what really hurts them. The extent of their hurt and wounds are not readily known by others. Angry people are more prone to discuss the faults and shortcomings of others rather than confront and disclose their own internal pain. When anger intervenes, problem solving is greatly compromised and, consequently, it is "hard to fix things."[24]

V. Ambivalence

Obviously, anger plays an integral role, in many ways, in the lives of bereaved survivors and their attempts at successful grief resolution. Yet, it doesn't end here. When one counterpoises all of the negative feelings that surface through anger with the positive ones that result from a loving relationship, a certain amount of ambivalence is manifested — strong positive and negative feelings may coexist. It would appear that the more that the positive and negative feelings exist in equal amounts, the greater will be the ensuing ambivalence. High ambivalence has the potential to complicate the grieving process. High ambivalence almost invariably generates an inordinate amount of guilt, which may frequently surface in the form of self-reproach. Guilt, such as — Was I a good wife? Did I do everything possible? Could I have done more? — is commonplace. This guilt that ensues can be a destructive force in successfully completing the journey toward healing.[25]

Guilt, its description and its ramifications and impact, is of consummate importance with respect to the successful resolution of the grieving process. To gloss over it would, indeed, be an injustice to the counselor and griever alike. Consequently, the role of guilt will be further explored in Chapter 12.

VI. Summary

A. Anger

1. Difficult Reaction

a. Lashing out indiscriminately

b. Nothing can please or soothe

c. Promotes rage and discomfort

2. Counterproductive and Destructive

B. Functional Role of Anger

1. To protect oneself from issues of fear and separation

2. Awareness of nature and purpose of hostile behavior

3. Need for attention and control

4. Disguise other emotions — depression, dependency

C. Survivor Resolution of Anger

1. Anger at deceased for having left them alone

2. "Regressive experience" — separation anxiety

3. Feelings must be qualified and directed accordingly

4. Anger channeled toward another living person

5. Anger directed inward

a. Depression

b. Suicidal Ideation

6. Anger for acts committed or omitted

a. Societal norms — say nothing negative of the dead

7. Anger "displaced onto" innocent people

D. Anger Can Result for Several Reasons

1. Feelings toward the loved one

2. How death occurred

E. Anger as Addictive

1. "Block" discomfort

2. Provides measure of control

F. Anger as Obstacle

1. Prevents "letting go"

2. Sets stage for unresolved grief

3. Problem solving compromised

G. Ambivalence

1. Positive and negative feelings

2. High ambivalence generates guilt

a. Guilt as a destructive force in grief resolution

Endnotes

[1] Elisabeth Kübler-Ross, *On Death and Dying* (New York: Macmillan Publishing Co., 1969).

[2] *Id.* at 50-51.

[3] *Id.* at 52.

[4] *Id.*

[5] *Id.* at 54.

[6] *Id.*

[7] Burl E. Gilliland, and Richard K. James, *Crisis Intervention Strategies* (California: Brooks/Cole, 1993), 409.

[8] J. William Worden, *Grief Counseling and Grief Therapy: A Handbook for the Mental Health Practitioner* (New York: Springer Publishing Co., 1982), 20.

[9] *Id.* at 20-21.

[10] *Id.* at 21.

[11] *Id.*

[12] Therese A. Rando, *How to Go On Living When Someone You Love Dies* (New York: Bantam Books, 1991), 29-30.

[13] *Id.* at 29-30.

[14] Worden, *supra* note 8, at 20-21.

[15] Rando, *supra* note 12, at 30.

[16] *Id.* at 30; Kevin Guinagh, *Dictionary of Foreign Phrases and Abbreviations* (3d ed.) (NewYork: H.W. Wilson Co., 1983), 50.

[17] Rando, *supra* note 12, at 31.

[18] Therese A. Rando, *Treatment of Complicated Mourning* (Illinois: Research Press Co., 1993), 467.

[19] *Id.* at 467-68.

[20] Matthew McKay, Peter D. Rogers, and Judith McKay, *When Anger Hurts: Quieting the Storm Within* (California: New Harbinger Publications Inc., 1989), 218.

[21] *Id.* at 218-20.

[22] *Id.* at 221.

[23] *Id.*

[24] *Id.* at 223.

[25] Worden, *supra* note 8, at 469, 478.

CHAPTER 12

The Role of Guilt

I. Introduction

One of the most enduring, and potentially harmful, aspects of the grief journey is the phenomenon of guilt. While most of the post-death guilt that mourner's experience is usually unsubstantiated and without merit, the effects nevertheless can seriously impede grief resolution.[1]

II. Factors of Guilt

When considering the role of guilt in grief resolution, it is important for the astute counselor to take into consideration a variety of factors, such as:

1. The level of ambivalence that may have existed in the survivor's relationship with the deceased (see Chapter 11).

2. The extent to which perceived guilt can endure reality testing. That is, does the griever have a substantial reason to feel guilty?[2]

3. How survivors can resolve real guilt.

4. The various types of guilt that survivors can manifest.

As indicated in Chapter 11, high ambivalence in a relationship almost invariably generates an inordinate amount of guilt that may frequently surface in the form of self-reproach. Guilt, such as — Was I a good wife? . . . Did I do everything possible? . . . Could I have done more? — is commonplace. The guilt that may ensue can be a destructive force in the successful completion of the journey toward healing.[3]

III. Guilt Resolution

Although most post-death guilt is, in actuality, unfounded,[4] the reality is that it does cause pain and must be dealt with. The most effective vehicle of guilt resolution in these cases is the use of reality testing: The survivor's pre-death behavior(s) must be objectively analyzed to determine if there is any substantive reason(s) to warrant or justify the perceived guilt. Frequently, concerns over acts of commission, as well as acts of omission, may haunt survivors and fuel feelings of guilt. The optimum result is that the guilt-ridden survivors will come to the realization that they did their best and, in reality, did no wrong.[5]

There will be times, however, when real culpability will emerge and real guilt will be felt. The resolution of this real guilt will be more complex. Survivors may benefit from interventions such as the exploration of their feelings of guilt; "empty chair" exercises in which feelings may be verbalized; "forgiveness" exercises; and, perhaps, cemetery (grave) visitations with follow-up processing.[6] It is imperative for school officials to remember, however, that these interventions must be left to qualified mental health practitioners and must not be attempted by laymen.

When one enters the realm of guilt, it must be done tactfully and with great caution. One must be keenly aware of the various types, causes, and even benefits that may accompany this all too common grief reaction. Because of its enormous potential for enduring and harmful residual effects, the phenomenon of guilt must be scrutinized and resolved in order to compliment and complete the grief resolution journey. Having done this, the survivor will be truly free to "let go" and reinvest in life.

IV. Problems to Be Explored

Before considering the actual types of guilt that may be experienced, the wise counselor would do well to examine just what guilt-related problems, left unresolved, can precipitate complicated mourning and thus jeopardize a successful grief resolution journey. One expert outlines five specific kinds of problems to be explored.[7]

1. In an effort to avoid guilt-producing thoughts, the mourner may opt to suppress certain recollections of the deceased as well as thoughts about the type of relationship that existed between them. This would allow the mourner to avoid confronting memories and feelings that might trigger feelings of remorse and guilt. "When the individual only processes the

positive aspects, mourning becomes skewed and incomplete."[8]

2. When a situation of unresolved guilt exists, the lack of resolution can impede the mourner's potential to accomplish any adaptive behaviors and to perpetuate bonds to past circumstances.[9]

3. Unresolved guilt may serve as a vehicle through which the mourner can remain connected to the loved one, to keep him or her "alive." The mourner may wish to resist guilt resolution in order to accomplish this. This may be prevalent following an inordinately ambivalent relationship. The guilt may be used to placate the deceased as well as to perpetuate any abuse that may have existed in the relationship.[10]

4. Problems ensue when the survivor employs guilt as a way of circumventing reality, an avoidance of the fact that this loss really did occur. It may be the survivor's way of refusing to let go of the loved one or of maintaining a sense that some benefit can be derived.[11]

5. In some cases, guilt may be used to camouflage other feelings and/or issues. It may serve to address specific mourner needs that require exploration and resolution. Left unresolved, these issues can impede grief resolution and precipitate complications.[12]

Significant guilt can result in punitive and other negative behavior(s).[13] Among these are depressed affect and suicidal ideation. In some cases, guilt may become much too overwhelming for the mourner to bear and may result in its being cast off or "projected" onto others within the mourner's immediate circle. This may include members of the nuclear family or even close friends. Needless to say, much confusion and disruption can ensue.[14]

V. Types of Guilt

Having explored some of the problems that may be posed by guilt, we will now examine several of the common kinds of guilt that may emerge as a result of any given death event.

Survivor's Guilt. When one survives a death event that others did not, a unique type of guilt emerges. This guilt may be a result of one's inability to accept the fact that he or she was powerless to prevent the death(s). Survivors often feel that they are to blame, that they could have done more to prevent the death. There may be an underlying assumption that the survivor, in fact, could have prevented the loss but didn't. There may even be a clandestine relief that the other person had died instead of the survivor. Victims of survivor's guilt often have difficulty accepting the fact that the conditions surrounding the loss may have been inevitable and that they were helpless to intervene. This is the case with natural disasters or acts of war. As cited in Chapter 2, parents may suffer from a devalued self-esteem at not having been able to protect the deceased child from the death event. They may, indeed, feel that they have failed as parents at not having done everything possible for the child.[15]

Guilt Resulting from Ambivalence. Sometimes in a close relationship both positive and negative feelings coexist.[16] This common, yet seemingly contradictory, situation often can lead to survivors' post-death feelings of guilt. These feelings are often intensified in the early stages of mourning when there is a normal tendency to idealize the deceased. In this setting, it can easily be perceived to be wrong, or even disloyal, to have entertained feelings of anger toward the loved one.[17]

With ambivalence in which positive and negative feelings exist in relatively equal amounts, significant guilt is usually generated as well as strong sentiments of anger at having been left behind and alone. Survivors frequently may question their performance in having done enough for the deceased loved one.

Functional Guilt. As with anger (see Chapter 11), guilt may at times be used to mask other, more crucial issues. It may serve a "protective function" by helping the survivor to avoid confronting an issue that may be threatening or that may produce anxiety.[18] The reader is directed to reconsider the story of Bob in Chapter 2. After several sessions, it was revealed that what Bob was really concerned with was separation anxiety. He was reluctant or afraid to say goodbye to his mother. His intense feelings of guilt, coupled with his equally intense refusal to part with even the slightest possession that she left behind, kept him so occupied that he didn't have the time or the presence of mind to confront the very real issue of having to say goodbye, forever, to his mother. His guilt served the function of protecting him from the even greater pain of taking permanent leave of his loved one. The separation anxiety was too much for Bob to bear.

Functional guilt must not be summarily stripped away.[19] The mourner must be able to identify the real underlying issue and deal with it in an adequate and therapeutic manner. Needless to say, this must be attempted only by a qualified mental health practitioner.

Contributory Guilt. The final kind of guilt to be explored in this discussion, but by no means the last kind of guilt that can be exhibited, deals with a form of self-reproach in which the survivor may believe that he or she may have actually contributed to the loved one's death, for example, the driver of the car in which the loved one was killed, the person who encouraged the deceased to participate in the activity that actually took his or her life, and the person who feels that they may be the one who actually caused the loved one's suicide. All of these individuals share the enormous burden of feeling that they, in fact, contributed to the loved one's death.[20] Adolescents may exhibit this form of guilt when they anguish over the possibility that perhaps, if some of their actions had been different, their loved one would not have died.[21]

Whatever the form of post-death guilt that is exhibited, it is important to remember that this guilt left unresolved can be harmful and enduring and a serious impediment to successful grief resolution. Equally important to remember is that unresolved grief must be treated only by a competent, professional mental health practitioner. Left untreated or improperly treated, unresolved guilt can cause unnecessary pain and can seriously impact the survivor's ability to resolve future losses. The death of a loved one can cause sufficient pain and anguish in and of itself. No one should have to endure more unnecessarily.

VI. Summary

A. Guilt Factors

    1. Level of ambivalence

    2. Perceived guilt and reality testing

    3. Resolution of real guilt

    4. Types of guilt

B. Ambivalence

    1. High ambivalence generates guilt

    2. Guilt may surface as self-reproach

C. Reality Testing

    1. Objectively analyze pre-death behaviors

    2. Existence of substantive reasons to warrant guilt

    3. Consideration of acts of commission and omission

    4. Realization of having done or not done wrong

D. Resolution of Real Guilt

    1. Exploration of feelings

    2. "Empty-chair" exercises

    3. Cemetery visitations with follow-up processing

    4. Interventions by qualified practitioners

E. Problems to Be Explored

    1. Suppression of certain recollections of deceased

    2. Lack of guilt resolution can impede adaptive behaviors

    3. Resisting guilt resolution to remain connected to deceased

    4. Use of guilt to circumvent reality

    5. Use of guilt to camouflage feelings and/or issues

F. Kinds of Guilt

    1. Survivor's guilt

2. Guilt resulting from ambivalence

3. Functional guilt

4. Contributory guilt

G. Importance of Guilt Resolution

1. Harmful and enduring if left unresolved

2. Reduce unnecessary pain

3. Assist resolution of future losses

4. Intervention by qualified mental health practitioner

Endnotes

[1] William J. Worden, *Grief Counseling and Grief Therapy. A Handbook for the Mental Health Practitioner* (New York: Springer Publishing Co., 1982), 42.

[2] *Id.*

[3] *Id.* at 30; Therese A. Rando, *Treatment of Complicated Mourning* (Illinois: Research Press Co., 1993), 469, 478.

[4] Worden, *supra* note 1, at 42.

[5] *Id.*

[6] Arthur E. Jongsma, Jr., and L. Mark Peterson, *The Complete Psychotherapy Treatment Planner* (New York: John Wiley and Sons, Inc., 1995), 70-71.

[7] Rando, *supra* note 3, at 483-84.

[8] *Id.* at 483.

[9] *Id.*

[10] *Id.* at 483-84

[11] *Id.* at 484.

[12] *Id.*

[13] *Id.*

[14] *Id.*

[15] *Id.* at 481; Therese A. Rando, (ed), *Parental Loss of a Child* (Illinois: Research Press Co., 1986), 421; Aphrodite Matsakis, *Posttraumatic Stress Disorder: A Complete Treatment Guide* (California: New Harbinger Publications, Inc., 1994), 181-82; Burl E. Gilliland, and Richard K. James, *Crisis Intervention Strategies* (California: Brooks/ Cole, 1993), 179; Michael E. Bernard, and Marie R. Joyce, "Rational Emotive Therapy with Children and Adolescents," in *Handbook of Psychotherapy with Children and Adolescents*, ed. Thomas R. Kratochwill and Richard J. Morris (Massachusetts: Allyn and Bacon, 1993) 239.

[16] Worden, *supra* note 1, at 30; Rando, *supra* note 3, at 480-81.

[17] See sources cited *supra* note 16.

[18] Rando, *supra* note 3, at 483.

[19] *Id.*

[20] *Id.* at 481.

[21] Laura Mufson, Donna Moreau, Myrna M. Weissman, and Gerald L. Klerman, *Interpersonal Psychotherapy for Depressed Adolescents* (New York: The Guilford Press, 1993), 91.

CHAPTER 13

Disenfranchised Grief

I. Introduction

One of the most psychologically and physically beneficial outlets of grief is the ability to express one's feelings — hurt, anger, rage, sadness, shock, desperation, emptiness, etc. — publicly. To face others and to be able to express one's anguish to others and with others somehow eases the pain. Someone else is sharing the tears and the hurt. One does not have to bear the burden alone, or does one? Until very recently, a phenomenon known as "disenfranchised grief" frequently robbed countless troubled mourners of the opportunity to jointly and publicly participate in the acceptance and resolution of their grief.

What is this disenfranchised grief? How could it have such a devastating effect upon one's misery? How can one define it?

Upon reflection, the writer remembers that early in his studies in Thanatology (the study of death and dying), one of his first teachers, Dr. Patrick Del Zoppo, gave a succinct definition. "Grief is a reaction to death, and mourning is when the grief has gone public."

In a general sense, in our society, people are free to react to their loss both privately and publicly. They are free to agonize, free to demonstrate their sorrow, and free to publicly give witness to their plight. However, sometimes circumstances (religious, moral, social, or even family-related) surrounding the death and/or the decedent compromise this freedom and compel certain survivors to withdraw from public manifestations of their loss. Their "right" to grieve publicly is unsanctioned; the privilege to do so is removed. Their right to public grief is disenfranchised, or as Doka (1989, p. 3) describes, "has little or no opportunity to mourn publicly."[1] Therefore, one can conclude that disenfranchised grief is one that, while being experienced, cannot be publicly expressed, mourned, or socially acceptable (Doka 1989, p. 4).[2]

In this chapter, the reader will find various common examples of this disenfranchised phenomenon and may even, in his/her own repertoire of experiences, find additional examples of a less common nature.

157

II. Occurrence of Disenfranchised Grief

By this point, it would appear the reader has a reasonable grasp of the nature of disenfranchised grief. One must now ask — When does it occur?

Doka (1989)[3] tells us that, in American society, the phenomenon of disenfranchised grief may surface in response to three basic reasons:

When the relationship between the decedent and the bereaved is not recognized.

The concept of disenfranchised grief may emerge when people of a non-kin relationship have intense feelings concerning the loss. Thus, co-workers, in-laws, friends, colleagues, etc., are expected, of course, to be supportive, however, they are not sanctioned to fully and publicly exercise an intense grief reaction. This is "supposed" to be reserved just for "family."

Additionally, there are other types of relationships that are not acceptable to the community at large. Participants in illicit sexual activities, extramarital encounters, or homosexual involvements, for example, may be socially prohibited from the full expression of their grief. They cannot sit with family and wail their pain. Children of such people also may be unable to fully externalize their feelings. Their grief may not be acknowledged nor publicly sustained.

Sometimes, even the loss of someone from a past "socially unacceptable" relationship may cause grief. However, the survivor's grief here, too, will find little public sanction. (Doka 1989, p. 5).[4]

When the *loss*, itself, fails to be recognized.

Sometimes a loss may elicit strong feelings of grief and sorrow, yet it may not be considered of such magnitude as to warrant a full grief scenario. A loss through miscarriage, while understood by all, may not be considered nearly as important as if an adult member of the family had died. Therefore, closest kin may have to resolve their grief in a very private sort of way (Doka 1989, pp. 5-6).[5]

Also counted among the innumerable disenfranchised grievers are those couples who, by their own decision and for whatever reasons, opted to have an abortion performed. Among certain ethnic and religious communities, having an abortion is equated to having taken a life and, consequently, the act carries a great stigma as well as ostracization. Obviously, these individuals do not feel free to approach their church, family, or friends for comfort. The psychosocial pressures that are exerted upon them ordinarily do not permit them to publicly vent their grief nor become members of a larger community of grievers. These people are largely left to fend for themselves emotionally and must sort out the pieces alone, as if they were a piece apart from the whole.

In recent times, horrific events such as mass shootings on school campuses or terrorist bombings have given rise to death situations in which the perpetrator has become so odious and disliked that to publicly honor his passing would almost amount to anathema. These people have done the unspeakable. They have taken innocent lives, a concept so unsanctioned by our society that the mere thought of paying respect, or affording dignity, to the perpetrator is most likely considered an assault on one's sensitivities. In cases like these, funeral activities are usually private and unobtrusive.

Doka (1989, p. 6)[6] mentions the death of a pet as an additional situation in which public expressions of grief may not be readily appreciated.

As a pet owner, himself, the author can emphatically state that the loss of a pet can be an extremely traumatic event for a person. The saving part of "pet grief" is that it is a much shorter experience than grieving for a human loss, and may often be overcome by the acquisition of a new pet.

Situations in which the *griever* may not ordinarily be recognized.

There are certain grief experiences in which individual grievers may be unrecognized or "left out." Doka (1989, pp. 6-7)[7] points out that this may happen when someone is perceived to be unable to comprehend the loss due to age, infirmity, or mental deficiency. In these cases the griever and his/her need to grieve may be overlooked.

III. Features of Disenfranchised Grief

By now it should be apparent that there must be some discernible features surrounding a loss that occurs from within a disenfranchised relationship. The reader would be wise to familiarize him/herself with these features in order to better understand and serve the sometimes disoriented survivors.

Hocker (1989)[8] identifies five features germane to the unsanctioned grief experience. They are offered here for the reader's consideration:

1. **Stigmatization:** When the survivor is aware of a gross lack of social sanction of the particular relationship, he/she not only suffers considerable embarrassment but is also uncomfortably reluctant to overtly display grief. One may be left with feelings of shame and face an incomplete support system at best (Hocker 1989, p. 263).[9]

2. **Inability to have funeral rituals:** Funeral rituals are an important part of grief resolution. They are the beginning of the journey toward healing, and when they are absent the recovery process may be seriously compromised (Hocker 1989, p. 264).[10] The funeral is one of the first opportunities for acceptance to take place, and acceptance is crucial to further progress.

3. **The timing of grief expression may be inappropriate:** Due to the very nature of unsanctioned grief, the disenfranchised griever may not be able to immediately begin the grieving process. It may have to begin at a later time, without drawing attention. However, the delay may be emotionally detrimental to the survivor (Hocker 1989, p. 264).[11]

4. **Financial and legal difficulties:** Problems such as these may often emerge when there is a financial dependency upon one member of an unsanctioned relationship. If this person died, the financial void would compound the loss. Likewise, litigation over property jointly shared by the decedent and the unsanctioned partner may affect the sense of loss and the recovery process (Hocker 1989, pp. 264-5).[12]

5. **Emotional complications:** If one were to compare all grief events or experiences, one would find certain characteristics that are common to all. However, in a disenfranchised situation, these features may be more pronounced. Feelings of frustration, guilt, anger, etc., may be intensified (Hocker 1989, p. 265).[13]

IV. Problems Specific to Unsanctioned Grief

Given the uniqueness of the variety of unsanctioned grief situations, it becomes apparent that these situations may be fraught with their own particular, special problems. Doka (1989)[14] speaks to this very point. One of the first things addressed is that, due to the nature of unsanctioned grief, the difficulty of mourning may be increased in various ways. As mentioned in Chapter 1, there are many reactions attendent to normal grief. However, Doka (1989, p. 7)[15] indicates that each unique circumstance of unsanctioned grief has the capacity to exacerbate the process. Doka goes on to cite the literature affirming that many of the feelings are intensified in situations of unsanctioned mourning (Doka 1989, p. 7).[16]

Another consideration is that ambivalence in a relationship (see Chapter 11) can be instrumental in directly affecting grief reactions, especially in the area of guilt. Ambivalence can be seen to exist among former spouses, among significant others in unsanctioned circumstances, and in instances of abortion (Doka 1989, p. 7).[17]

As mentioned earlier, one of the many problems that emerge from an unsanctioned grief scenario is the inability of some of the bereaved to be active participants in the final rites for the decedent. Unfortunately, the disenfranchised griever cannot be a final caretaker for the loved one, nor can he/she participate actively in the funeral rituals that are usually very instrumental in heralding the beginning of grief resolution. Indeed, sometimes there is no way that the unsanctioned griever can actively and meaningfully mourn the loss (Doka 1989, p. 8).[18]

V. Expected Social Support in a Bereavement Context

While the purpose of this chapter is to impart to the reader a grasp of some of the mechanics that may come into play in an unsanctioned grief scenario, it would, nevertheless, be useful to conclude with a brief overview of some of the desired modes of support that all mourners do need. Rando (1993) summarizes these nicely:

1. **Presence** — Mourners appreciate someone being there for them.

2. **Emotional Encouragement** — Mourners need someone to help them to process feelings.

161

3. **Emotional Validation** — Mourners need someone to acknowledge the pain of their loss.

4. **Instrumental or Logistical Support** — Survivors need someone to help with arrangements, daily tasks, cooking, etc.

5. **Informative/Directional Support** — The direction that survivors need to process the proper information concerning the death event.

6. **Relationship and Intimacy Support** — The survivors need someone to be, "the rock" for them during their time of need.

7. **Social Intervention** — The survivors need to be diverted from grief, given a respite, and helped to reinvest in life.

(Rando 1993, pp. 495-6)[19]

VI. Summary

A. Disenfranchised Grief

1. Grief cannot be overtly, publicly expressed

2. The individual may not be socially sanctioned to grieve

3. Circumstances surrounding death may compromise freedom to mourn

B. Occurrence of Disenfranchised Grief

1. When the relationship between the decedent and the bereaved is not recognized

2. When the loss, itself, fails to be recognized

3. Situations in which the griever may not ordinarily be recognized

C. Features of Disenfranchised Grief

1. Stigmatization

2. Inability to have funeral rituals

3. The timing of grief expression may be inappropriate

4. Financial and legal difficulties

5. Emotional complications

D. Problems Specific to Unsanctioned Grief

1. Some of the unique characteristics of unsanctioned grief may actually exacerbate the process

2. Feelings may be intensified in the course of unsanctioned grief

3. Ambivalence may affect grief reactions

4. Exclusion from care-giving and funeral rituals

E. Expected Social Support in a Bereavement Context

1. Presence of others

2. Emotional encouragement

3. Emotional validation

4. Instrumental or logistical support

5. Informative/Directional support

6. Relationship and Intimacy support

7. Social intervention

Endnotes

[1] Kenneth J. Doka, ed., *Disenfranchised Grief: Recognizing Hidden Sorrow* (Massachusetts: Lexington Books, 1989).

[2] *Id.*

[3] *Id.*

[4] *Id.*

[5] *Id.*

[6] *Id.*

[7] *Id.*

[8] William V. Hocker, *Unsanctioned and Unrecognized Grief: A Funeral Director's Perspective in Disenfranchised Grief: Recognizing Hidden Sorrow*, edited by Kenneth J. Doka (Mass.: Lexington Books, 1989).

[9] *Id.*

[10] *Id.*

[11] *Id.*

[12] *Id.*

[13] *Id.*

[14] Doka, *supra* note 1.

[15] *Id.*

[16] *Id.*

[17] *Id.*

[18] *Id.*

[19] Therese A. Rando, *Treatment of Complicated Mourning* (Illinois: Research Press Co., 1993).

CHAPTER 14

Memorialization

I. Introduction

One of the most poignant, and potentially therapeutic, experiences following the death of a loved one is the act of memorialization. Not infrequently, this may be an integral part of the actual funeral ritual(s), although some families may prefer to have a memorial event as a separate service apart from the funeral itself. Whichever course survivors choose to follow, memorialization may be seen as the first step in the grief resolution process and is, thus, significant. For the purpose of this chapter, the terms *funeral* and *memorialization* will be used synonymously.

As suggested in preceding chapters, the death of a loved one often results in an idealized conceptualization of the deceased. This idealization often is helpful in the verbalization of feelings that may have always existed, but, perhaps, existed in silence. The memorial to the loved one is often guided, and may even be dominated, by the survivors' need to adequately display respect for the deceased.

It is important to bear in mind the admonition given in Chapter 8 with respect to a death by suicide. A suicide death can present a unique problem with respect to inadvertently glorifying the deceased. Great care must be exercised so as not to encourage "copycat" or "cluster" suicides. While it is important for school officials to address the situation with information, it is best to do so without undue personal displays of emotion. The role of the School Bereavement Team is to recognize and acknowledge the pain and sorrow and to help ease the grief.[1] In the case of the altruistic suicide, undue glorification may equate the act to martyrdom and, thus, may make the act appealing to other distressed students.

II. The Value of Memorialization

The value, or role, of the funeral (memorialization) service is as a form of catalytic agent to successful grief resolution. One of the immediate benefits of the memorialization is that it helps the bereaved to accomplish the first of the four tasks of grief — the acceptance of the reality of the loss.[2] When the survivors participate, they are confronted with the indisputable fact that this death has really occurred. This is particularly poignant and apparent when viewing the loved one in an open casket.

Rituals are vehicles for the expression of one's innermost emotions and cognitions.[3] They provide a unifying factor that can result in a value- and belief-based support system. The funerary ritual provides a socially acceptable public forum that permits survivors to openly express their pain, thoughts, and grief at the loss of their beloved. It is a culture-based component of one's immediate support system. The funeral can be seen as a facilitator in the realization and overt expression of the survivors' feelings as well as the entrance into experiencing the pain of the loss.[4]

Memorialization is vital to the grieving process in that it can provide the opportunity for the survivor to process his or her own experiences and relationship with the deceased and, perhaps, even share this legacy with others.[5] Frequently, the memorialization will contain a personalized component that will eulogize or reflect upon the life of the deceased. More frequently in recent times, other members of the grieving community may take active roles in the ceremony.[6] The memorialization ritual may truly become a celebration of the beloved's life. The mutual sharing that occurs is instrumental in the affirmation of the esteem the mourners have for the deceased and the validation of their pain.[7]

The memorialization process also can be seen as an adjunct to the survivors' struggle to adjusting to life without the deceased, in their effort to create a "new self-identity." Public memorials give the survivors the opportunity to step into this new identity and afford the community the opportunity to recognize this new dimension and offer appropriate support.[8]

III. Types of Memorializations

For all of these reasons, memorialization holds a privileged position on the continuum of the grief resolution journey. It is important; it is meaningful; and it is efficacious.

When school officials are suddenly confronted with the loss of life within the school community, they also may be confronted with what type of memorialization would be appropriate. The choices may vary from elaborate public dedications to more modest, individual activities. The wise school administrator will try to tailor the memorial event to fit each particular occasion. It may be useful to consider a few sample memorializations.

As mentioned earlier, memorialization may frequently occur during the course of the funeral ritual itself. If so, the nature of, and participants in, the event may be determined by the loved one's family and/or the presiding clergy. The nature and extent of memorialization also may be determined by the flexibility of religious and cultural considerations. One expert suggests that clergy be consulted to help ensure that the needs of the bereaved are adequately met.[9]

Memorial services, apart from funerary rituals, also are a frequent choice for honoring the deceased. In an academic setting, memorials may take place in the school auditorium or other suitable place. The service also may include a dedication of some sort, for example, a gymnasium, a library, or a particular room. As with funerals, care should be exercised to include mourners and provide for their needs. Family members, friends, and school personnel may be called upon to take part in a lasting tribute to the loved one. It is important to remember that funerals and memorials have the capacity to bring about aspects of grief resolution.[10]

Frequently, a variety of other activities may be used that can provide for greater participation among the mourners and still allow them to contribute meaningfully, even eloquently, to the lasting memory of a beloved friend.

Memorial Wall. Wall space can be designated where students may post letters, pictures, or poems that will help to ease their grief and to facilitate the pleasant memory of the deceased student and friend.[11] As one researcher states, "corporate sharing seems to facilitate healthy grieving."[12]

Scrapbooks. Grieving students should be encouraged to compile individual scrapbooks in which they can gather drawings, poems, photos, and stories about the deceased to depict aspects of his or her life.[13]

Scholarships. The school can establish a scholarship in memory of the deceased member of the school community to perpetuate the name and memory and to pay tribute to the individual person.[14]

167

Monetary Donations. Students can collect money to support a special interest of the loved one. These donations may be made to charities, shelters, clubs, or interest groups in memory of the lost loved one.[15]

Volunteering Services. When an elaborate and impressive memorial is deemed unwise, as in the case of a suicide death, students can express their regard for the deceased by volunteering their time and services in activities designed to benefit the living. Students may staff telephones at crisis centers, become peer tutors, or give their time in other meaningful ways to reflect their love and esteem for a deceased friend.[16]

Whatever the form that memorialization may take, it is important that school officials realize its importance in helping the family and the bereaved move past their grief. Memorials are beneficial in that they provide a socially acceptable, public forum to proclaim one's grief, share one's pain, and reach out to another in support and consolation.

School officials must strive to provide memorials that meet the age-specific needs of their students and other members of the school community. It takes patience, sympathy, empathy, and creativity, but it can be done. For the welfare of the students, it must be done. Memorialization is vital in that it can set the stage and tone of the healing process. Properly done, it can stimulate mourners' resolve to make the journey from pain to healing, from anguish to a cherished memory. It is the first step, but it is a crucial one.

IV. Summary

   A. Memorialization

      1. A potentially therapeutic experience

      2. May be integrated into the funeral service

      3. May be held as a separate service

      4. The first step in the resolution of grief

   B. Reasons for Memorialization

      1. To confront the reality of the death

2. To verbalize thoughts and feelings

3. To adequately display respect for the deceased

C. The Value of Memorialization

1. A catalytic agent in grief resolution

2. Acknowledges that death has really occurred

3. A unifying factor

4. A socially acceptable forum for the public expression of pain and grief

5. A culture-based component of one's immediate support system

6. An entrance into experiencing the pain of the loss

7. An opportunity for survivors to process experiences and relationships with the deceased

8. A celebration of the beloved's life

9. Emergence of survivors' new self-identity

10. Community recognition of the new self-identity

11. Memorialization is important, meaningful, efficacious

D. Types of Memorializations

1. Dignified, formal service of reflection and celebration

2. Memorial service in conjunction with a dedication

3. Memorial wall

4. Scrapbooks

5. Scholarships

6. Monetary donations

7. Volunteering Services

Endnotes

[1] Patrick W. McKee, R. Wayne Jones and Richard H. Barbe, *Suicide and the School: A Practical Guide to Suicide Prevention* (Pennsylvania: LRP Publications, 1993), 84-85.

[2] J. William Worden, *Grief Counseling and Grief Therapy. A Handbook for the Mental Health Practitioner* (New York: Springer Publishing Co., 1982), 11; see also Chapter 4.

[3] Alan D. Wolfelt, "Creating Meaningful Funeral Ceremonies Part II: Exploring the Purposes of Meaningful Funeral Ceremonies." *Thanatos* 19, no. 4 (1994): 4-8.

[4] Therese A. Rando, *Grief, Dying, and Death: Clinical Interventions for Caregivers* (Illinois: Research Press Co., 1984), 181; Wolfelt, *supra* note 3, at 6; Worden, *supra* note 2, at 50-51.

[5] Wolfelt, *supra* note 3, at 6.

[6] Worden, *supra* note 2, at 51.

[7] Wolfelt, *supra* note 3, at 6. *Id.* at 6-7.

[8] *Id.* at 6-7.

[9] Rando, *supra* note 4, at 195.

[10] *Id.* at 192.

[11] Louise M. Aldrich, "Sudden Death — Crisis in the School," *Thanatos* 20, no. 3 (1995):13.

[12] Martha D. Oates, *Death in the School Community A Handbook for Counselors, Teachers, and Administrators* (Virginia: American Counseling Association, 1993), 45.

[13] Aldrich, *supra* note 11, at 13; Oates, *supra* note 12, at 45.

[14] See sources cited *supra* note 13.

[15] Oates, *supra* note 12, at 45.

[16] *Id.*

APPENDIX A

Sample Correspondence

Memorandum Issued Following the Death of a Student

Date_____

From: Principal's Name

To: All Members of the Faculty

All members of the professional staff are asked to make the following announcement during the homeroom period this morning:

Dear Students,

I have the unpleasant task of informing you that one of your fellow classmates, _____, died yesterday as a result of _____. The entire school community joins you in mourning this loss.

I realize how upset you must be and I will arrange for bereavement counselors to be available to speak with you. If you want to speak with one of these counselors, please notify me. Passes with the time of appointment will be issued to you during homeroom period.

When all arrangements have been finalized, the complete information will be posted on the main bulletin board.

Let us all join in a moment of silence in _____'s memory.

Thank you.

171

Memorandum Issued Following the Death of a Teacher

Date_____

From: Principal's name

To: All Members of the Faculty

All members of the professional staff are asked to make the following announcement during the homeroom period this morning:

Dear Students,

It is my sad duty to announce to you that Mr(s)._____, one of our beloved teachers, died last night as a result of_____.

Mr(s)._____dedicated_____years of [his or her] life to teaching the students here at_____School, and I am sure that [he or she] will be greatly missed.

When all arrangements have been finalized, the complete information will be posted on the main bulletin board in the school lobby.

Let us all join in a moment of silence in his or her memory.

Thank you

Letter Issued to Parents Following the Death of a Student

The following letter may be sent to parents following the death of a student. It may be altered to reflect any specific type of death, such as suicide, accident, or homicide.

Dear Parent,

It is my sad duty to inform you of the death of one of our students, _____, due to _____.

We at _____School are very much concerned with the students' reactions to this sad event. In order to help students adjust to this loss, I have arranged for bereavement specialists to be on hand to speak with our students should they request it. In addition, I am in the process of arranging for support groups for both students and parents. Details will be announced as soon as possible.

In the interim, please do everything possible to support your child and make yourself available to discuss this event with him/her. In the event that your child may need more immediate attention, please call me at [contact number].

In order to help you to better assess each individual situation, I have taken the liberty of enclosing material that describes some of the normal grief reactions that may occur following a significant loss.

Please be assured that, together, we can do everything possible to help your child through this difficult period.

Sincerely yours,

Principal

Encl.

APPENDIX B

Sample Permission Forms

Notice of School-Based Bereavement Support Groups and Permission Form

Dear Parent,

As a response to concern following the untimely death of _____, the school community has arranged for on-site bereavement support groups to be led by trained specialists. Students are invited to participate and discuss various aspects of grieving, the healing journey, as well as the various determinants and tasks of grief. It is our hope that these sessions will do much to alleviate the tension, doubts, and fears that may often accompany the loss of a loved one.

If you would like your child to participate in one of these bereavement support groups, please be so kind as to sign the permission form below and have your child return it to his/her homeroom teacher. Please be advised that these groups will be scheduled so as not to conflict with regular class instruction.

I will be available to speak with you should you have any questions or concerns. You may reach me at_____.

Sincerely yours,

Principal

Date:_____

I, _____give my son/daughter
_____of class_____ permission to participate in
the school-based bereavement support group. I understand that the
group sessions will be programmed so as to avoid the loss of regular
instructional time.

Signature of Parent_____

Telephone No._____

Note: Please remember that legal requirements will vary from venue
to venue and a call to the school district legal desk is advised prior to
finalizing a valid permission document.

Permission Form

Date:_____

To Whom It May Concern,

I, _____parent of _____, hereby give my son/ daughter permission to participate in a school-based bereavement support group to be offered at _____School.

I understand that this support group will be scheduled for a time that will not conflict with regular instructional time.

Parent Signature_____

Telephone No._____

State of_____

County of_____

Sworn to before me this_____ day of _____, 19_____

Notary Public_____

Affix Official Seal

Note: Please remember that legal requirements will vary from venue to venue and a call to the school district legal desk is advised prior to finalizing a valid permission document.

APPENDIX C

Grief Resolution Inventory

Instruction: Think about the death you experienced. Place a check in the blank under your answer to each question.

Most of the time	Some of the time	Not at all or rarely	
_____	_____	_____	1. Can you talk about this loss without becoming upset?
_____	_____	_____	2. Can you think about how your life was before this loss without feeling a great deal of emotional pain?
_____	_____	_____	3. Do you feel angry, either at a specific person or just angry in general, when you think of this loss?
_____	_____	_____	4. Are you generally happy and look forward to the future and the good things it will bring you?
_____	_____	_____	5. Can you go places that remind you of this loss without being overly upset or feeling depressed?
_____	_____	_____	6. Do you still think or say "If only. . ." about this death?
_____	_____	_____	7. Do you remember this person's good points and his/ her bad ones?
_____	_____	_____	8. Do you feel guilty about your prior relationship with this person or about any of the events that caused the death?

Reprinted from "Death in the School Community: A Handbook for Counselors, Teachers, and Administrators" by Martha D. Oates, Ed.D., © 1993. *Reprinted by permission.*

179

Score your inventory as follows:

a. Assign three (3) points for each check under "most of the time" for questions 1, 2, 4, 5, and 7. _____

b. Assign three (3) points for each check under "not at all or rarely" for questions 3, 6, and 8. _____

c. Add one (1) point for each check under "some of the time." _____

Total: _____

A score of 18-24 usually means that a person is experiencing a healthy resolution of grief. Anyone who scores below 18 may profit from participation in a grief support group. A score below 12 may indicate a need for grief counseling.

APPENDIX D

Key Differences Between Grief and Depression

Experience of	Grieving	Depression
Loss	There is a recognizable loss by the bereaved.	There may not be a recognizable loss by the depressed, or the loss is seen as punishment.
Mood states	Quickly shifts from sadness to more normal state in same day. Variability in mood, psychomotor activity, level, verbal communication, appetite, and sexual interest within same day/week.	Sadness mixed with anger. Tension or absence of energy. Consistent sense of depletion, psychomotor retardation, anorexia with weight loss; sexual interest is down, verbal communication is down; or agitation, compulsive eating, sexuality or verbal output.
Expression of anger	Open anger and hostility.	Absence of externally directed anger and hostility.
Expression of sadness	Weeping.	Difficulty in weeping or in controlling weeping.
Dreams, fantasies, and imagery	Vivid, clear dreams, fantasy, and capacity for imagery, particularly involving the loss.	Relatively little access to dreams; low capacity for fantasy or imagery (except self-punitive).
Sleep disturbance	Disturbing dreams; episodic difficulties in getting to sleep.	Severe insomnia, early morning awakening.
Self-concept	Sees self as to blame for not providing adequately for lost object. Tendency to experience the world as empty. Preoccupation with lost objects or person.	Sees self as bad because of being depressed. Tendency to experience self as worthless. Preoccupation with self. Suicidal ideas and feelings.
Responsiveness	Responds to warmth and reassurance.	Responds to repeated promises, pressure, and urging or unresponsive to most stimuli.

181

| Pleasure | Variable restrictions of pleasure. | Persistent restrictions of pleasure. |
| Reaction of others to affected person | Tendency to feel sympathy for griever, to want to touch or hold the person who is grieving. | Tendency to feel irritation toward depressed. Rarely feels like touching or reaching out to depressed. |

Reprinted with permission from *Pastoral Bereavement Counseling. A Training Program for Caregivers in Ministry to the Bereaved* by Patrick M. Del Zoppo, ©1993 by the Archdiocese of New York.

Developmental Ages and Possible Reactions to Death

Age	Think	Feel	Do
3-5 years (preschool)	• death is temporary and reversible • finality of death is not evident • death mixed up with trips, sleep • may wonder what deceased is doing	• Sad • Anxious • Withdrawn • Confused about the changes • Angry • Scared • Cranky (feelings are acted out in play!)	• Cry • Fight • Are interested in dead things • Act as if death never happened
6-9 years	• about the finality of death • about the biological processes of death • death is related to mutilation • a spirit gets you when you die • their actions and words caused the death	• Sad • Anxious • Withdrawn • Confused about the changes • Angry • Scared • Cranky (feelings are acted out in play!)	• Behave aggressively • Behave withdrawn • Experience nightmares • Act as if death never happened • Lack concentration • Have a decline in grades
9-12 years	• about and understand the finality of death • death is hard to talk about • that death may happen again, and feel anxious • about death with jocularity • about what will happen if their parent(s) die • their actions and words caused the death	• Vulnerable • Anxious • Scared • Lonely • Confused • Angry • Sad • Abandoned • Guilty • Fearful • Worried • Isolated	• Behave aggressively • Behave withdrawn • Talk about physical aspects of death • Act as if it never happened, not show feelings • Experience nightmares • Lack concentration • Have a decline in grades
12 years and up (teenagers)	• about and understand the finality of death • if they show their feelings they will be weak • they need to be in control of their feelings • about death with jocularity • only about life before or after death • their actions and words caused the death	• Vulnerable • Anxious • Scared • Lonely • Confused • Angry • Sad • Abandoned • Guilty • Fearful • Worried • Isolated	• Behave impulsively • Argue, scream, fight • Allow themselves to be in dangerous situations • Grieve for what may have been • Experience nightmares • Act as if it never happened • Lack concentration • Have a decline in grades

Reprinted with permission from "Sudden Death — Crisis in the School," by L.M. Aldrich in *Thanatos*, vol. 20, iss. 3, page 11, ©1995 by Florida Funeral Directors Services, Inc.

183

Variables of Childhood and Adolescent Loss

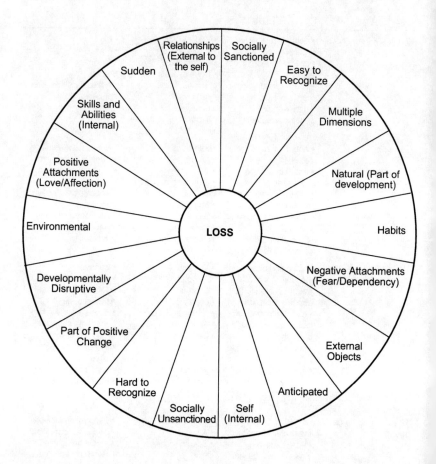

Reprinted with permission from *Growing Through Grief: A K-12 Curriculum to Help Young People Through All Kinds of Loss,* ©1989, Compassion Books, 477 Branch Road, Burnsville, North Carolina. (828) 675-5909.

BIBLIOGRAPHY

Aldrich, Louise M. "Sudden Death — Crisis in the School." *Thanatos*, 20, no. 3 (1995).

Barker, Robert L. *The Social Work Dictionary*. 2d ed. Washington, D.C.: The NASW Press, 1991.

Becker, Ernest. *The Denial of Death*. New York: The Free Press, 1973.

Bernard, Michael E. and Marie R. Joyce. "Rational Emotive Therapy with Children and Adolescents." In *Handbook of Psycho-therapy with Children and Adolescents*, edited by Thomas R. Kratochwill and Richard J. Morris. Massachusetts: Allyn and Bacon, 1993.

Bluestone, Joyce. "School-Based Peer Therapy to Facilitate Mourning in Latency-Age Children Following Sudden Parental Death." In *Play Therapy with Children in Crisis*, edited by N.B. Webb. New York: The Guilford Press, 1991.

Bowlby, John. *Attachment and Loss: Loss, Sadness, and Depression* (Vol. III). New York: Basic Books, 1980.

Bruno, Frank J. *Psychological Symptoms*. New York: John Wiley and Sons, Inc., 1993.

Craig, Grace J. and Riva Specht. *Human Development: A Social Work Perspective*. New York: Prentice Hall, 1987.

Deaton, Robert L. and William A. Berkan. *Planning and Managing Death Issues in the Schools: A Handbook*.

Del Zoppo, Patrick M. *PASSAGES: A Guidebook for TEENS in GRIEF — their Parents, Friends, and Caregivers*. Patrick Del Zoppo Associates, New York: The Richmond Institute, 1993.

Del Zoppo, Patrick M. *Pastoral Bereavement Counseling: A Training Program for Caregivers in Ministry to the Bereaved*. New York: Archdiocese of New York, 1993.

Del Zoppo, Patrick M. *To Be Lifted Up: The Journey from Grief to Healing*. New York: Archdiocese of New York, 1989.

Diagnostic and Statistical Manual of Mental Disorders. 4th ed. Washington, D.C.: American Psychiatric Association, 1994.

Doka, Kenneth J., ed. *Disenfranchised Grief: Recognizing Hidden Sorrow*. Massachusetts: Lexington Books, 1989.

Fishman, Charles H. *Treating Troubled Adolescents: A Family Therapy Approach*. New York: Basic Books, Inc., 1988.

Fox, Raymond. *Elements of the Helping Process: A Guide for Clinicians*. New York: Haworth Press, 1993.

Gentry, Doyle W. *Anger-Free: Ten Basic Steps to Managing Your Anger*. William Morrow and Co., Inc. New York, 1999.

Germain, Carel B. *Human Behavior in the Social Environment*. New York: Columbia University Press, 1991.

Gilliland, Burl E. and Richard K. James. *Crisis Intervention Strategies*. California: Brooks/Cole, 1993.

Goodman, Robin F. "Diagnosis of Childhood Cancer." In *Play Therapy with Children in Crisis*, edited by N.B. Webb. New York: The Guilford Press, 1991.

Greenstone, James L. and Sharon C. Leviton. *The Elements of Crisis Intervention*. California: Brooks/Cole, 1993.

Greenwood Press, Westport, Connecticut, 1995.

Greist, John H., M.D. and James W. Jefferson, M.D. *Dealing with Depression: Taking Steps in the Right Direction*, Pfizer, U.S. Pharmaceuticals Group, New York, 1996.

"Grieving the Loss of a Loved One." In *Crisis Intervention Handbook: Assessment, Treatment, and Research*, edited by A. Roberts. California: Wadsworth, Inc., 1990.

Guinagh, Kevin. *Dictionary of Foreign Phrases and Abbreviations*. 3d ed. New York: H.W. Wilson Co., 1983.

Hocker, William V. *Unsanctioned and Unrecognized Grief: A Funeral Director's Perspective in Disenfranchised Grief: Recognizing Hidden Sorrow*, edited by Kenneth J. Doka. Mass.: Lexington Books, 1989.

House, Alvin E. *DSM-IV Diagnosis in the Schools*. The Guilford Press, New York, 1999.

James, John W. and Frank Cherry. *The Grief Recovery Handbook: A Step-by-Step Program for Moving Beyond Loss*. New York: Harper and Row, 1988.

Jongsma, Arthur E. Jr. and L. Mark Peterson. *The Complete Psychotherapy Treatment Planner*. New York: John Wiley and Sons, Inc., 1995.

Kaplan, Bert. "Anxiety States." In *Adult Psychopathology: A Social Work Perspective*, edited by F.J. Turner. New York: The Free Press, 1984.

Kaplan, Harold 1. and Benjamin J. Sadock. *Pocket Handbook of Emergency Psychiatric Medicine*. Baltimore: Williams and Wilkins, 1993.

Kastenbaum, Robert. *The Psychology of Death*. 2d ed. New York: Springer Publishing Co., Inc., 1992.

Kastenbaum, Robert. "Time and Death in Adolescence." In *The Meaning of Death*, edited by H. Feffel. New York: McGraw Hill, 1959.

Keller, Martin B., George M. Simpson, Alan F. Schatzberg, and Myrna M. Weissman. *Learning to Live with Depression*, Medicine in the Public Interest, Inc. (MIPI), Boston, 1994.

Klugman, David J., Robert E. Litman, and Carl I. Wold. "Suicide: Answering the Cry for Help." In *Differential Diagnosis and Treatment in Social Work*, edited by F. Turner. New York: The Free Press, 1983.

Kübler-Ross, Elisabeth. *On Death and Dying*. New York: Macmillan Publishing Co., 1969.

Kübler-Ross, Elisabeth. *Questions and Answers On Death and Dying*. New York: Macmillan Publishing Co., 1974.

Landis, Judson R. *Sociology: Concepts and Characteristics*. 8th ed. California: Wadsworth Inc., 1992.

Lewis, Robin, Betty A. Walker, and Marilyn Mehr. "Counseling with Adolescent Suicidal Clients and Their Families." In *Crisis Intervention Handbook: Assessment, Treatment, and Research*, edited by A. Roberts. California: Wadsworth, Inc., 1990.

Lilly, Eli and Co. S*imply live: A Guide to Your Recovery*, PW-22092, Eli Lilly and Company, Indiana, 2001.

Liotta, Alfred J. "My First Crisis: How A Counselor Could Have Helped My Family." *Thanatos* 20, no. 2 (1995).

Malcolm, Andrew H. *Thunder Across the Land*, "Notre Dame Magazine," Indiana, Vol. 30, No. 4, Winter 2001-02.

Mancini, Mary Elizabeth. "Creating and Therapeutically Utilizing Anticipatory Grief in Survivors of Sudden Death." In *Loss and Anticipatory Grief,* edited by T. Rando. Mass.: D.C. Heath and Co., 1986.

Matsakis, Aphrodite. *Post-Traumatic Stress Disorder: A Complete Treatment Guide*. California: New Harbinger Publications, Inc., 1994.

McConville, Brian J. "Assessment, Crisis Intervention, and Time Limited Cognitive Therapy with Children and Adolescents Grieving the Loss of a Loved One." In *Crisis Handbook: Assessment, Treatment, and Research*, edited by A. Roberts. California: Wadsworth, Inc., 1990.

McKay, Matthew, Peter D. Rogers, and Judith McKay. *When Anger Hurts: Quieting the Storm Within*. California: New Harbinger Publications, Inc., 1989.

McKee, Patrick W., R. Wayne Jones, and Richard H. Barbe. *Suicide and the School: A Practical Guide to Suicide Prevention*. Pennsylvania: LRP Publications, 1993.

Miles, Margaret S. and Alice S. Derni. "Guilt in Bereaved Parents." In *Parental Loss of a Child*, edited by T. Rando. Illinois: Research Press Co., 1986.

Mishne, Judith Marks. *Clinical Work with Adolescents*. New York: The Free Press, 1986.

Mufson, Laura, Donna Moreau, Myrna M. Weissman, and Gerald L. Klerman. *Interpersonal Psychotherapy for Depressed Adolescents.* New York: The Guilford Press, 1993.

Nagy, Maria. 'The Child's View of Death." In *The Meaning of Death,* edited by H. Feifel. New York: McGraw Hill, 1959. (Original work published 1948.).

Oates, Martha D. *Death in the School Community. A Handbook for Counselors, Teachers, and Administrators.* Virginia: American Counseling Association, 1993.

Pangrazzi, Arnaldo. "Overcoming Grief. Ten Suggestions," St. Anthony Messenger (Reprint), January, 1983.

Pfizer Inc. *Zoloft: for the Treatment of Depression.* 23-5712-00-2, TL565X99, Pfizer; U.S. Pharmaceuticals, New York, 2000.

Pine, Vanderlyn R. and Carolyn Brauer. "Parental Grief: A Synthesis of Theory, Research, and Intervention." In *Parental Loss of a Child,* edited by T. Rando. Illinois: Research Press Co., 1986.

Price, Jane E. "The Effects of Divorce Precipitate a Suicide Threat." In *Play Therapy with Children in Crisis,* edited by N.B. Webb. New York: The Guilford Press, 1991.

Rando, Therese A. ed. *Parental Loss of a Child.* Illinois: Research Press Co., 1986.

Rando, Therese A. *Grief, Dying, and Death: Clinical Interventions for Caregivers.* Illinois: Research Press Co., 1984.

Rando, Therese A. *How to Go on Living When Someone You Love Dies.* New York: Bantam Books, 1991.

Rando, Therese A. *Treatment of Complicated Mourning.* Illinois: Research Press Co., 1993.

Robbins, Dennis A. "Legal and Ethical Issues in Terminal Illness Care for Patients, Families, Caregivers, and Institutions." In *Loss and Anticipatory Grief,* edited by T. Rando. Massachusetts: D.C. Heath and Co., 1986.

189

Rudd, David M. and Thomas Joiner and M. Hasan Rajab. *Treating Suicidal Behavior: An Effective, Time-Limited Approach.* Guilford Press, New York, 2001.

Saravay, Barbara. "Short-Term Play Therapy with Two Pre-school Brothers Following Sudden Paternal Death." In *Play Therapy with Children in Crisis*, edited by N.B. Webb. New York: The Guilford Press, 1991.

Schoenberg, B.M. ed. *Bereavement Counseling. A Multidisciplinary Handbook.* Connecticut: Greenwood Press, 1980.

Shulman, Lawrence. *The Skills of Helping. Individuals, Families, and Groups.* Illinois: Peacock Publishers, 1992.

Stahl, Lori. "Music Therapy and the Grieving Child." *Thanatos* 15, no. 3 (1990).

Turner, Francis J. ed. *Differential Diagnosis and Treatment in Social Work.* 3d ed. New York: The Free Press, 1983.

Webb, Nancy Boyd. ed. *Play Therapy with Children in Crisis.* New York: The Guilford Press, 1991.

Webster's New World College Dictionary, Fourth Edition, ©2000, 1999 by IDG Books Worldwide, Inc., California.

Wolfelt, Alan D. "Creating Meaningful Funeral Ceremonies Part II: Exploring the Purposes of Meaningful Funeral Ceremonies." *Thanatos* 19, no. 4 (1994).

Wolfelt, Alan D. "Helping Children Cope With Grief." *Thanatos* 16, no. 3 (1991).

Wolfelt, Alan D. "Toward an Understanding of the Going Crazy Syndrome." *Thanatos* 17, no. 3 (1992).

Worden, J. William. *Grief Counseling and Grief Therapy: A Handbook for the Mental Health Practitioner.* New York: Springer Publishing Co., 1982.

INDEX

A

Acceptance of loss, 8, 36–37, 53–54
Action checklist, 17–22
Active euthanasia, 120
Adjustment disorder with depressed mood, 95
Adjustment to new environment, 8, 37, 54–55, 83–84
Adolescents, bereavement, 75–89
    characteristics of, 75–76
    danger signs for, 79–80
    interventions for, 80
    posttraumatic stress disorder in, 79, 122, 136
    reaction to death by, 76–79
    6-session model for, 80–86
Altruistic suicide, 110
Ambivalence, 44
    anger and, 144–145
    disenfranchised grief and, 161
    guilt from, 152
    suicide and, 112
American Academy of Crisis Interveners Lethality Scale, 111–112
Anger
    in adolescents, 78
    ambivalence and, 144–145
    in children, 65
    pre-death, 141
    as reaction, 141
    reasons for, 143–144
    role of, 141–146
    survivor resolution of, 142–143
    terrorism and, 132–133
Anomic suicide, 110
Art therapy, 69

B

Behavioral therapy, 99–100
Bereavement counseling
    action checklist, 17–22
    effective, 8–10
    support group, 10–17
Bereavement program
    facilities for, 3
    materials for, 4
    parental notification and consent for, 5–6
    for parents, 27–39
    procedures for, 6–8, 28–29
    resources for, 4–5
    staff for, 3–4
    for students, 3–8
    team for, 4, 28
Biological theory, 96

C

Cathexis, 8, 37, 55–56
Chemotherapy, 100–101
Children. *See also* Adolescents
    bereavement of, 63–72
    death of, 29–30, 32–35
    development of, 63–65
    intervention guidelines, 67–70
    needs of, 65–66
    posttraumatic stress disorder in, 122, 136
Cognitive theory, 96–97
Cognitive therapy, 100
Complicated mourning, 12, 121
Consent of parents
    need for, 5–6

need for, 5–6
sample, 175

O

Oates, Martha, 17
On Death and Dying, 141

P

Pain of grief, experiencing, 8, 37,
54
Pangrazzi, Arnaldo, 31
Parents
bereavement programs for,
27–39
consent of, 5–6
death of child, 29–30, 32–35
determinants of grief for, 35–
36
middle-age, characteristics
of, 29–32
notification of, 5–6
tasks of grief for, 36–37
Permission forms, sample, 176–177
Pharmacological intervention, 100–
101
Play therapy, 67–70
Posttraumatic Stress Disorder
(PTSD)
in adolescents, 79, 122, 136
in children, 122, 136
factors contributing to, 123
in homicide survivors, 121–
124
symptoms of, 121–122, 136
terrorism and, 135–136

in traumatic death survivors,
121–124
treatment of, 122–123
Professional mourners, 46
Program. *See* Bereavement program
Protection of Pupil Rights Amend-
ment Act (PPRA), 5
Psychoanalytic theory, 96
Psychotherapy, 99–100
PTSD. *See* Posttraumatic Stress
Disorder (PTSD)
Puppet play, 68

R

Reactions to grief, 1–2. *See also*
Anger; Guilt; Posttraumatic
Stress Disorder (PTSD)
by adolescents, 76–79
by children, 64–65
in homicide, 120–124
by survivors of suicide victims, 113–114, 119
in traumatic death, 120–124

S

Sand play, 69–70
Scholarships, 167
School Bereavement Team, 4, 28,
165
Scrapbooks, 167
Selective Serotonin-Reuptake
Inhibitors (SSRIs), 100–101
Shock, 6, 77–78
Shock treatment, 101
Stigmatization, 160
Storytelling, 15, 69, 81